ENDORSEMENTS

Thanks to Pam and CJ for giving their hearts and time to develop a study on character based on Ruth, one of the great stories in all the Bible of the value of a commitment to character. While I know this is a natural fit for many women's Bible studies, it's also a great study for a couples group or even a men's group. (Men, you can call it a study of Boaz if that'll help!) In a day in which character is something we must fight for, this study in Ruth will give groups the strength and direction to fight well.

Tom Holladay
Associate Senior Pastor, Saddleback Church

Tossed, Tumbled and Still Trusting is an exceptional Bible study on multiple levels. A great devotional work must of course have exercises that bring out the Bible's relevance to contemporary needs and longings, and it must be capable of leading the reader to life-changing decisions for the better. CJ and Pam have provided a wealth of material for these purposes, both for individuals and for groups. But when I evaluate devotional studies, I often find a disconnect between what the biblical text actually teaches and what the author claims it teaches. To get it right, we have to put ourselves in the sandals of the original audience and understand the text from their perspective. CJ and Pam have done that by providing the historical background to the book of Ruth, not in the dry language of a formal commentary, but in simple, heart-felt terms that do not leave the reader bored or asking, "So what?" I'm also impressed by the fact that the authors tackle the tough issues; for example, none is tougher than the relationship between God's sovereignty and human free will. As difficult as these issues are, I don't know how any author can be intellectually honest in an endeavor of this kind without dealing with them. I look forward to seeing many more works of this quality.

Don Wilkins, Th.M., Ph.D.
Scholar in Residence, The Lockman Foundation

CJ Rapp and Pam Marotta skillfully draw lessons from the life of Ruth that give us a creative and engaging graduate course in refining our character. In a world where character is more a literary term than an ethical one, we greatly need this fresh approach to the study of Ruth to help us develop the Christ-like qualities that give us the character to live a life of ultimate fulfillment and real success.

Shelley Leith
Co-author of *Character Makeover*

Tossed, Tumbled and Still Trusting will challenge the reader to the truth of what God clearly desires of us: Christ-like character. CJ and Pam, thank you for elucidating this truth so eloquently.

Sandra Maddox
Author of *Tiffany and the Talking Frog* and contributing writer of *Chicken Soup for the Soul: Grieving and Recovery*

We loved *Tossed, Tumbled and Still Trusting!* This study on Ruth was in-depth, vibrant, and fresh. The women in our group loved discussing the character issues faced by Naomi and Ruth. Their tests and trials are very similar to what we experience today. We felt encouraged and loved as CJ authentically shared her life throughout the lessons. The study was relevant in its content and we were inspired to face each new challenge trusting that God would give us something precious through it—more of him! Every week we left strengthened, stirred and full of faith to face whatever life had to offer. We have been forever changed!

Charli Mack, Group Facilitator
Heart 2 Heart, First Presbyterian Church, Monrovia, CA

Tossed, Tumbled and Still Trusting

A STUDY IN THE BOOK OF RUTH

CJ Rapp

and

Pam Marotta

A Bible Study from:
The University of Refining Our Character (UROC)

Infusion
P·U·B·L·I·S·H·I·N·G
A Ministry of Unfading Beauty Ministries

Edited by Teresa Haymaker

Infusion Publishing™
Mission Viejo, CA 92692

Infusion Publishing is a ministry of Unfading Beauty Ministries.
www.unfadingbeautyministries.org
Phone: 949-954-4237

First edition   July 2011

ISBN: 0-9824790-3-4
Printed in the United States of America

Unless otherwise noted, Scripture quotations are taken from the NEW AMERICAN STANDARD BIBLE®, © Copyright 1960, 1962, 1963, 1968, 1971, 1972, 1973, 1975, 1977, 1995 by The Lockman Foundation. Used by permission. (www.Lockman.org)

Scripture quotations marked AMP are from the Amplified® Bible, Copyright © 1954, 1958, 1962, 1964, 1965, 1987 by The Lockman Foundation, Used by permission. (www.Lockman.org)

Scripture quotations marked GNT are from the Good News Translation–Second Edition, © 1992 by American Bible Society. Used by Permission.

Quotations marked NIV are from the Holy Bible, New International Version®. Copyright © 1973, 1978, 1984, by International Bible Society. Used by permission of Zondervan Publishing House. All rights reserved.

Quotations marked KJV are taken from the King James Version of the Bible.

Quotations marked NLT are taken from the Holy Bible, New Living Translation, copyright © 1996. Used by permission of Tyndale House Publishers, Inc., Wheaton, IL 60189. All rights reserved.

Scripture quotations marked NRSV are from the NEW REVISED STANDARD VERSION of the Bible. Copyright © 1989. Used by permission of the Division of Christian Education of the National Council of Churches of Christ in America.

Scripture quotations marked The Message are copyright © by Eugene H. Peterson 1993, 1994, 1995, 1996, 2000, 2001, 2002. Used by permission of NavPress Publishing Group.

Layout by Teresa Haymaker
Cover Design by Suzana Stankovic

DEDICATION

For Every Woman...

ACKNOWLEDGEMENTS

We would like to thank Teresa Haymaker for all the hard work, advice, and expertise she generously shared with us through the process of compiling this book. Your friendship is priceless, as are you!

We also want to thank the Heart 2 Heart Women's Group at First Presbyterian Church in Monrovia, California. Your friendship and willingness to be our pilot group for *Tossed, Tumbled and Still Trusting* means so much to us! You all blessed us with your feedback and love. We appreciate your part in making this study in the Book of Ruth stronger. A special thanks to Charli; we appreciate your love, support, and friendship.

CJ's –

I would also like to thank the women of La Jolla Community Church. Your retreat was the inspiration for this study. You are amazing women.

Thank you Debbie Eaton for affirming the direction of this study and encouraging me to pursue it!

My writing partner Pam, the Lord has blessed me with your friendship and mentorship through the years. You will never know how much I love you. Thank you for being a Ruth to me!

Finally to my children, Dillon and Austin, and my husband, John, thank you for supporting the hours writing this study required. I am so thankful for all of you—especially you John. You never let me give up on the dream God placed in my heart. When I doubt or encounter hardship you encourage me to keep going. I love you so much!

Pam's –

I want to thank a few of those who have encouraged and helped me in my journey to become the writer I am today. Without your influence I wouldn't be writing Bible studies. Many thanks to Steve Gladen, Brett Eastman, Allen White, Tom Holladay, Rob DeKlotz, Robyn Henk, Teresa Haymaker, Peggy Rose, and of course, CJ Rapp, my writing partner. I am truly blessed to have served the Lord with all of you—I will always treasure your friendship and the memories of our times together in ministry!

CJ, you are truly one of God's gifts to me. Your friendship and love always touch my heart. I am continually challenged in my spiritual journey as we work together writing these Bible studies. I love how God uses us together and I thank him for putting you in my life!

I don't know what I would do without my wonderful husband, David. My life would not be the same without your love, caring, and unfailing support. Thank you for always causing me to feel cherished and protected, for encouraging me, and putting up with my long hours of writing! I love you always!

CONTENTS

WELCOME

Welcome to *Tossed, Tumbled and Still Trusting—A Study in the Book of Ruth.*

UROC is an acronym for University of Refining Our Character. We have taken some principles of university life and terminology to create a Bible study curriculum series with a different twist. UROC is a series of Bible studies designed to facilitate refining the believer's character. Our prayer is that, through this format, God will use the lessons as the means for his transforming work in your life.

We are pleased to introduce *Tossed, Tumbled and Still Trusting—A Study in the Book of Ruth.* It is the first study in the UROC Series. Each of the nine lessons are designed using three assignments for each lesson. For a detailed understanding of what to expect from this exciting new study see *Using Your Study Guide* for details.

Thank you for choosing UROC's *Tossed, Tumbled and Still Trusting.* We are confident you will be pleased as you work through this life-changing study.

CJ would love to hear from you. You can contact her at cj@cjrapp.com. And you can visit her website at www.cjrapp.com.

HOW TO USE YOUR STUDY GUIDE

We are excited you have joined us and we pray that you find this study to be a memorable part of your spiritual journey.

As you look through your *Tossed, Tumbled and Still Trusting* study guide you will notice that not every lesson looks identical. We've chosen to offer something for everyone by varying the kinds of exercises, questions, and skills we provide for you. We hope you find this approach fun and interesting. Don't be afraid to take on new things—you may find a new approach that is really fun for you! If you don't like some things, that's okay, since we are offering you variety and we may not use that technique subsequently.

THE FORMAT

ONE LESSON—THREE ASSIGNMENTS: Each week you will study one lesson. Each lesson includes three assignments. These assignments address one or two principles covered in the lesson. You can study one assignment a day, all three in one day, or break up the study time in any way that works for your schedule.

SOMETHING TO THINK ABOUT: This section includes commentary by CJ on what you have studied as well as offering some things she wants you to think about a little more. Take time to read them because this is where she might challenge you the most.

BOXED NOTES: These notes are important concepts we don't want you to miss. They might include a Word Study, a verse of Scripture, a study skill to add to your learning, or just a thought to reinforce what you are studying.

WRAPPING IT UP: Here CJ will offer her comments and thoughts about the main ideas to take away from each lesson. This is a good place to step back and take a minute or two to think back over what you have studied—to think about how it applies to your everyday life. *Wrapping it Up* will help refocus the big picture of the lesson and remind you that the goal of your Bible study is to transform your life. Don't be overwhelmed, God doesn't change you all at once—take hold of one principle each week and ask God to show you one intentional step you can take toward becoming more like him.

EXTRA CREDIT: You may find an Extra Credit question occasionally; they are optional, of course. These questions may not have simple answers and they may only be a "What do you think?" question. They are designed to challenge your thinking a bit. Don't be afraid to guess if you want to. You won't be put on the spot to share your thoughts. Experienced Bible students may find these to be fun and thought-provoking.

APPLICATION FOR REVIEW: This section is designed to help you process the timeless principles you glean from the Scriptures you study and apply them to your life. Some weeks you will find this section devoted to application and other weeks the application will be sprinkled throughout the lesson.

STUDY GROUP QUESTIONS: When you attend a university you may find joining a "study group" to be helpful. Your small group or break-out group is your study group—a group of those who are like-minded and committed to studying the same curriculum and sharing the learning experience together.

Since most small group meetings do not allow enough time to discuss all the questions you study throughout the week, we have provided several questions at the end of the lesson to help you focus your group's discussion. These questions will direct your discussion on one or two key points from each assignment. For additional ideas for leading your group discussion see the *Leader Guide* in the *Appendix*.

APPENDIX: Your appendix is somewhat like your book-bag or backpack. It's the place where you store everything you might need while you meet with your study group or study on your own. Here is where we have stored resources that will help your study. Check it out—some things you'll use a lot and some things you may use only once. Some things you'll find there are:

- **LEADER GUIDE:** This section will help both experienced and inexperienced leaders find a comfortable flow for guiding the group time together. You'll find some help and ideas for handling questions that might be difficult. Also, we offer ideas for leading through a discussion that fits the specific needs and experience of your group.

- **OBSERVATION SHEET:** The observation sheet is the text of the entire Book of Ruth from the *New American Standard Bible* (NASB). Use it to highlight, underline, make notes in the margins, write lists of things you are learning, or mark in any way you desire. Of course you can use your own Bible or any good translation, but the observation sheet is available in the *Appendix* if you choose to use it.

- **ADDITIONAL RESOURCES:** You will also find other resources designed to enhance individual lessons. Be sure to check them out!

LESSON ONE:

Prerequisite

Most upper level college courses require a prerequisite. A prerequisite is defined as study required before taking the desired course. In this case we must first understand the back story of Ruth—the historical events surrounding the time, the culture, the political climate, and the family structure. This is important because it provides context. Context aids in our understanding of the Scriptures we study.

The Book of Ruth is set in the time of the Judges, 1373-1051 BC. God's people, Israel, had been delivered from captivity in Egypt. They were led through the wilderness for forty years by Moses. Upon Moses' death Joshua led Israel into the Promised Land. The Lord gave them victory over their enemies, enabling them to live in the land that God had promised them through Abraham. However, God had instructed Israel to drive out the inhabitants of the land; instead they allowed their enemies to remain and live among them. In time, Joshua died leaving Israel without a righteous leader who remembered the deeds and deliverance the Lord had given them. This plunged the nation into a time of confusion and turmoil. God then raised up righteous men and women to serve as judges—leaders placed over the people.

Assignment One

Let's begin our study by reading what God has to say through the Scripture regarding the time of the Judges. Read Judges Chapter 2 to see a picture of what was going on with the Israelites and their relationship with God.

1. Look again at verses 10-13 and 19-22 on the next page. Write down how these verses present the Israelite's relationship with God.

10　*All that generation also were gathered to their fathers; and there arose another generation after them who did not know the Lord, nor yet the work which He had done for Israel.*

11　*Then the sons of Israel did evil in the sight of the Lord and served the Baals,*

12　*and they forsook the Lord, the God of their fathers, who had brought them out of the land of Egypt, and followed other gods from among the gods of the peoples who were around them, and bowed themselves down to them; thus they provoked the Lord to anger.*

13　*So they forsook the Lord and served Baal and the Ashtaroth. Judges 2:10–13*

19　*But it came about when the judge died, that they would turn back and act more corruptly than their fathers, in following other gods to serve them and bow down to them; they did not abandon their practices or their stubborn ways.*

20　*So the anger of the LORD burned against Israel, and He said, "Because this nation has transgressed My covenant which I commanded their fathers and has not listened to My voice,*

21　*I also will no longer drive out before them any of the nations which Joshua left when he died,*

22　*in order to test Israel by them, whether they will keep the way of the LORD to walk in it as their fathers did, or not." Judges 2:19–22*

2.　Look up and read the following verses from Judges. After reading each verse, consider what you learned about the times and culture the people lived in during the period of the Judges and fill in the blanks below.

<u>Scripture</u>	<u>What was happening?</u>
Judges 3:7	They did what was evil in the sight of the LORD, _____ the Lord their God and _____ the Ba'als and the Asheroth.
Judges 10:6	Then the sons of Israel again did _____ in the sight of the LORD, _____ the *Ba'als* and the Ashtaroth... thus they _____ the LORD and did not _____ Him.
Judges 17:6	The people did what was _____ in their own eyes.

3.   Briefly summarize what you have learned about the time of the Judges.

4.   Judges 17:6 says, *In those days there was no king in Israel; every man did what was right in his own eyes.* What do you think it means for a person to do *what [is] right in their own eyes?*

5.   How is the time in which we live today similar to the time of the Judges?

Something to Think About:

We live in a society that encourages us to do what is "right in our own eyes." Slogans like *Just do it!* and the cultural mentality that says "I have to do what is right for me," convince us that it's okay to choose instant-gratification and self-gratification over God's way. This mentality makes us think we are masters of our own destiny. Unfortunately decisions made apart from God lead us down godless roads that end in pain and loss.

Assignment Two

In *Assignment One*, we learned that during the time of the Judges the people did what was right in their own eyes. But we also saw in Judges 2:10 that the righteous generation died and the new generation did not know the Lord or the wonderful work he had done on their behalf. The New Living Translation gives us further insight into what it means to not know the Lord:

> 10 *After that generation died, another generation grew up who did not <u>acknowledge</u> the LORD or remember the mighty things he had done for Israel.* (NLT)

While this verse could imply that the older generation failed to tell of God's great work on behalf of Israel, it could also mean the younger generation suffered from unbelief thus rejecting the Lord's grace toward them and their responsibilities toward him.

Friends, as we look closely at the Book of Ruth, ask yourselves how different life might have been throughout the generations if the people had been faithful to pass down their faith and share stories of God's deliverance on their behalf.

Today we begin our study on the Book of Ruth. Remember the Book of Ruth is set in the time of the Judges.

1445 BC – 1440 BC		1405 BC	1373 BC – 1051*
Exodus from Egypt	Moses leads Israel through the wilderness	Joshua leads the people into the Promised Land	Judges rule Israel
Dates are taken from The History of Israel New Inductive Study Bible.			

1. Before we start to look closely at the details of the Book of Ruth we need to see the big picture. This is called an overview. An overview is a survey of the major content of the book being studied. We are not looking at details yet. Instead we are looking for the big pieces that make up the whole. Take time now to read the entire Book of Ruth; you'll find it in the *New American Standard Bible* (NASB) translation located in the *Appendix* or you can read it in your own Bible. Read it as you would a letter from a friend. Try to read it in one sitting if possible. (Take heart—it's only four chapters!)

2. Record your thoughts about the story. What stands out the most? Be sure to record the verses where your thoughts come from.

3. Briefly summarize the Book of Ruth.

4. Extra Credit: In light of what you have learned about the era of the Judges and from what you have read in the Book of Ruth, write a quick summary of what you understand the culture was like in Bethlehem when Naomi left with her family to live in Moab.

5. Look up the following words in an English dictionary and write out the meaning for each one as they apply in the Book of Ruth. If you don't own a dictionary consider using an online dictionary. We recommend www.dictionary.com.

    •   Famine

    •   Return

- Glean

- Redeem

Something to Think About:

Imagine living in a time of great lack; a time when people are short on hope and in desperate need. Sounds like the times we live in today doesn't it? I can't help but wonder how different the culture Ruth lived in might have been had the people been diligent to remember the deeds and work of the Lord in their recent past. How different would our experience be if we habitually remembered God's goodness in the past during our current trials?

Assignment Three

In *Assignment Two* we took a look into the setting of Ruth. We met the key people in the Book of Ruth—Naomi, Ruth and Boaz. We explored the time in which they lived; a time characterized by famine and people doing what was right in their own eyes. We are almost finished with *Lesson One*. Before you begin today's assignment take a look back at the definitions you looked up last time. Did you have any new insights into the meanings of the words? Did anything grab your attention?

1. Quickly scan the Book of Ruth located in the *Appendix* and underline or highlight the following words. Record the verse references and what you learn about the words below. We've given you some hints to get you started.

- Famine (i.e. Where was it? Who was affected by it?)

- Return (i.e. Who said it? Why?)

> **Note Taking Tips**
>
> When marking key words that you want to find easily later, it is helpful to use bright colors and underlining, circles, or boxes around the text so that they stand out.

- Glean

- Redeem

2. Extra Credit: Why do you think the Book of Ruth was included in the Bible based only on your first reading? If you have no idea, that is okay; we'll look to find the answer as we go along.

   (There is more than one possible explanation so don't be afraid to make a guess at this point!☺)

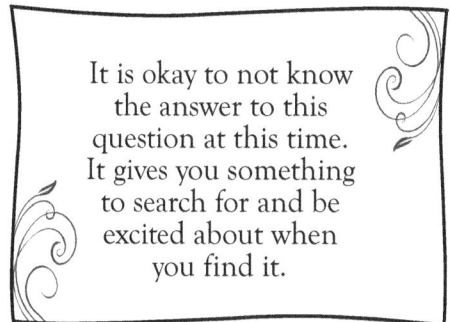

> It is okay to not know the answer to this question at this time. It gives you something to search for and be excited about when you find it.

Something to Think About:

Note in the space below anything interesting you saw as you searched the Scriptures for the words above. Is there anything you want to learn more about? If so, make sure you remember to check back here throughout the study to see if you have discovered the answers to your questions.

Wrapping it Up:

Well friends, you've completed the study portion of the first lesson. I encourage you to meditate on the words of Ruth you read this week. What is God speaking to you about? What similarities do you see in the lives of the people then and of people today? Really, we are not that different. Yes, society is different, and so is technology, but deep down inside we are all very much alike. I hope you are seeing how relevant this Old Testament book is to our lives today. If you don't see it yet, don't worry because as the study unfolds your insight will become clearer.

Application for Review

1. Circle the phrase that best completes the following statement: I want to be a person who:

    *   does what culture tells me is right.

    *   does what is right in God's eyes.

    *   does what it is right in my own eyes.

    How close are you to being that kind of person?

    When I think about what it means to do what is right in my own eyes, I can't help but think about all the decisions I have made throughout my life. At every fork in the road there was a choice. A choice to seek God in prayer or through his Word and then to act in obedience or choose to simply do what felt right in the moment. It was easy to do what felt right. It was more difficult to wait on God for direction and guidance. To do what is right in your own eyes really is to be driven by the flesh and its desires. To do what is right in God's eyes is to surrender to his Spirit and his will for your life.

    My questions are simply this: "How are you doing with surrendering your will to his will?" "Does doing what is right in God's eyes feel stifling or freeing to you?" "Does it frighten you or embolden you?" Explain your answers. Consider writing a prayer to God asking him to help you consistently overcome the desire to do what is right in your own eyes and follow him.

2. Briefly review your work for this week. Try to identify any timeless principles you see in the character of the people, from events or circumstances that might be considered relevant to our culture today. Record your thoughts here.

> A *timeless principle* is an important fact; a consequential or influential truth that applies today as it did when it was written.

3. Spend some time in prayer; ask God what you can apply to your life from this lesson. If possible, write down one next step or a change you can make to align your life with God's desires for you.

4. What has God shown you that you would like to explore further during our study in the Book of Ruth?

5.   In Judges 2:10 we learned how important it is to remember the work of the Lord in our lives. In the space below describe one test, trial or triumph and how God worked on your behalf. Describe what happened, how God brought you through it, and what you learned from it.

6.   Challenge: Can you think of someone who would be encouraged in their circumstance by hearing your story of God's faithfulness? Take a step of faith and share with them this week.

Study Group Questions

1.   How does doing what is right in our own eyes differ from doing what God desires? Give some examples to support your answer.

2.   Do you think there are consequences for doing what is right in your own eyes today? Why or why not?

3.   How can we know what is right in God's eyes?

4.   What, if anything, did you find interesting about the words: famine, return, glean, and redeem?

5.   What in this lesson is most significant to you and why?

NOTES

LESSON TWO:

University of Refining Our Character

A university is an institution for learning and growth. During the course of this study we will liken our journey in Christ to a time of training in a university, the university where our character is refined into the likeness of Christ. UROC stands for *University of Refining Our Character*. UROC is our analogy to the Christian life. In other words, while most universities are 4-8 years of study, UROC is a lifetime learning institution. We are likening graduation to the day Jesus calls us home. Our graduation ceremony takes place in heaven and our graduation gifts include the crown of life, hidden manna, and a white stone with a new name on it. (James 1:12, Rev. 2:17).

The goal of UROC is found in Romans 8:

29 *For God knew his people in advance, and he chose them to become like his Son, so that his Son would be the firstborn among many brothers and sisters.* Romans 8:29 (NLT)

At UROC our goal is a transformed life that reflects the character of Christ. God loves us just as we are, but he loves us too much to leave us the way we are. He wants us to grow and mature in faith. So once we become followers of Christ he sends us through UROC. A student's life in a university requires focused learning, understanding, and intentional application of the things learned. In UROC these are also true.

You don't have to go away to attend this university because life itself is the university. Life is a series of tests. Every challenge, trial, heartache, tragedy, and victory is an opportunity for us to grow and mature in our character. In fact, look at what James 1:2-4 in The Message translation says:

2-4 *Consider it a sheer gift, friends, when tests and challenges come at you from all sides. You know that under pressure, your faith—life is forced into the open and shows its true colors. So don't try to get out of anything prematurely. Let it do its work so you become mature and well-developed, not deficient in any way.*

The trials and tests of life teach us lessons about God and faith. God is constantly at work through the experiences of life—teaching us, guiding us, and shaping our character to reflect his son. Through each experience we learn to overcome our flesh and desires, to respond as Christ would. Our growth is not just internal; it becomes external—obviously visible to those around us.

> Our growth is not just internal; it becomes external—obviously visible to those around us.

The goal of UROC is Christ-likeness in all tests, trials, and tragedies. In order to grow and mature in Christ we must learn to overcome the impulses and desires of the flesh.

Let's begin our study for this week by looking at the challenges faced in Ruth 1:1-5.

Assignment One

The Book of Ruth is an excellent example of the tests and challenges of life. The way we react to each test or trial in life reveals our character. It reveals what is in our hearts. God is more interested in our character than he is our comfort. Why? Because the only thing we take to eternity is our character. As you read Ruth 1:1-5 notice the challenges that Elimelech's family faced.

Write down what you observe. We have given you some hints below.

Observation

1. What do you see in verse 1 that reveals when this story took place?

We have all seen commercials or stories on television about famine in foreign lands. The pictures of hungry faces tug at our hearts. What feelings do you think the famine evoked in the people?

2. Who were the governing authorities during the time of this story according to verse 1?

   How do you think the people's concept of God or relationship with God was affected by the famine and hardships they were facing?

3. Who are the main characters mentioned in verses 1 and 2, and what do you learn about them?

4. List the challenges and tragedies the family experienced. How were their experiences similar to what people face today?

5. Look back at *Lesson One* on page 5 where you recorded the English definition of the word famine. How does the definition help you to understand what was happening in Bethlehem while Elimelech and Naomi lived there?

6. What decision did Elimelech and Naomi make as a result of the famine (lack) in verses 1 and 2?

7. Look up the word "sojourn" from verse 1 in an English dictionary and compare it with the word "remained" in verse 2. Why might these words represent significant decisions in Naomi's life?

Something to Think About:

In the first five verses of the Book of Ruth we see the realities of life. The ups and downs, the love and loss, joy and sorrow, triumph and tragedy, and finally, forks in the road that require decisions to be made. Some things are within our control and others are not.

Our life experiences are not really different today. There is always a new test or challenge that comes our way. The question is how do you consistently respond to those experiences? How we respond reveals the true state of our character. How could having an intimate relationship with God help your response to each new test and trial?

Assignment Two

In *Assignment One* we learned that Elimelech and his family left Bethlehem in Judah to escape the famine. Remember that Elimelech and Naomi lived in Bethlehem of Judah. Bethlehem means "house of bread." Bethlehem was in the Promised Land, a land given to Israel by God. These were God's chosen people living in the land flowing with milk and honey. But they were experiencing very difficult times. They were also living in the times of the Judges when people did what was right in their own eyes and did not know the Lord or remember his great deeds. Today, we'll examine the reasons for the family's decision to leave Bethlehem.

1. Compare the information on Moab below with Deuteronomy 23:3-6 and Judges 17:6 to help you understand more about the times and circumstances Elimelech and Naomi found themselves living in. Record any interesting thoughts you have gained below. Be sure to record the verses you are referencing along with your thoughts.

Moab

The Moabites were distant relatives of the Israelites. They were descendents of Lot through the incestuous relations with his oldest daughter (Genesis 19:30-38). In Deuteronomy 23:3-4 the Moabites were banned from the congregation of the Lord for ten generations. God gave two reasons for this ban. First, the Moabites refused Moses' request for the Israelites to pass through Moabite land as they traveled from Egypt to the Promised Land (Judges 11:17). Secondly, the King of Moab called on Balaam, son of Beor, to curse Israel as they went into battle (Numbers 22:4-6). Needless to say the Moabites were considered enemies of Israel.

---

2. Naomi and Elimelech's sons' names may hold some significance since, in their culture, names did reflect something significant about a person. Mahlon means sickly, and Chilion means pining or wasting. If their names truly reflect the kind of people the sons were, how might this have influenced their decision to move from Bethlehem to Moab?

3. Judges 2:10 describes the spiritual condition of Israel as a time when people did not know (acknowledge) the Lord or the works he had done on Israel's behalf. How do you think this truth affected Elimelech's decision to leave Bethlehem?

Famine is defined as an extreme lack. Not only were the people of Bethlehem experiencing a physical famine, they were experiencing a spiritual famine. Instead of turning to the Lord, praying and trusting for his provision, Elimelech looked for sustenance outside the boundaries of the Promised Land. In effect, he looked to the world to meet his needs. When you experience lack where do you turn? Do you look to God for the provision you need for this day or do you turn to the world? The world and what it offers can never meet your need. We must learn to look to God to supply all our needs.

In Matthew 6, Jesus says:

31   *Do not worry then, saying, "What will we eat?" or "What will we drink?" or "What will we wear for clothing?"*

32   *For the Gentiles eagerly seek all these things; for your heavenly Father knows that you need all these things.*

33   *But seek first His kingdom and His righteousness, and all these things will be added to you.*
     Matthew 6:31–33

I know these words are hard to hear when we are in the midst of trials and tragedies. But our circumstances and how we feel about them don't make them less true. The Father knows what we need before we ask, but understanding and believing this truth comes from intimately knowing God and seeing him meet the needs in your life. God commanded Israel to remember the great deeds he had done for them, to live by his commands, and to teach them to their children. Read Deuteronomy 6:6-12:

6   *These words, which I am commanding you today, shall be on your heart.*

7   *You shall teach them diligently to your sons and shall talk of them when you sit in your house and when you walk by the way and when you lie down and when you rise up.*

8   *You shall bind them as a sign on your hand and they shall be as frontals on your forehead.*

9   *You shall write them on the doorposts of your house and on your gates.*

10   *Then it shall come about when the Lord your God brings you into the land which He swore to your fathers, Abraham, Isaac and Jacob, to give you, great and splendid cities which you did not build,*

11   *and houses full of all good things which you did not fill, and hewn cisterns which you did not dig, vineyards and olive trees which you did not plant, and you eat and are satisfied,*

12   *then watch yourself, that you do not forget the Lord who brought you from the land of Egypt, out of the house of slavery.*

4.   How do you think Elimelech's choice to leave Bethlehem might have been different if the *Lord's* commands in Deuteronomy 6:6-12 had been consistently practiced throughout the generations?

> When we practice this Scripture we will see life through God's provision instead of from our lack.

5.   Why is it important to remember and to speak of the deeds the Lord has done on your behalf?

Something to Think About:

There is a direct connection between our spiritual growth and remembering the deeds of the Lord. The more we see him at work in our lives, the more we are able to trust him when we are faced with trials and tribulations. Trust in God and his provisions is an essential lesson of UROC. Without this trust we will never learn to be consistent over-comers of our own fleshly desires and temptations. Likewise, the way we respond to our challenges will be affected by the degree to which we trust him. Like the Israelites, if we forget to rely on God and his provisions, we'll be in danger of making godless decisions that lead us outside the will of God and his best for us. How are you recording and proclaiming God's provision and work in your life?

Assignment Three

In *Assignment Two*, we explored the decision Elimelech made to leave Bethlehem in Judah and the possible motivation for his decisions. Today we'll look at how we grow as a result of the trials and troubles of life. Remember life is the university, the tests we experience reveal our character. Job was a man who experienced many trials and tragedies in life. In the midst of his tragedy he expressed this simple hope:

> 10 *But He knows the way I take;*
>
> *When He has tried me, I shall come forth as gold.* Job 23:10

Why don't we pray this together? *Lord you know the way I take, after you have tried me I shall come forth as pure gold.*

1. Read Ruth 1:1–5 and record the events and circumstances Naomi experienced.

   Based on what you learned so far, how do you think Naomi's decisions and responses to each event reveals her true character, good or bad?

EVENT OR DECISION	CHARACTER QUALITY
1:1	
1:2	

Event or Decision	Character Quality
1:3	
1:4	
1:5	

2. Life here on Earth is the University of Refining Our Character. Using the table below, list key events in your life that have had the greatest influence on your character. How satisfied are you with your response to the circumstance? How do you think you grew as a result of those circumstances?

Your Life Experience or Circumstance	What You Learned from the Experience or Circumstance

3. In the Book of Revelation the word "overcomes" is an important characteristic associated with believers. Revelation 2:17 says, *He who has an ear, let him hear what the Spirit says to the churches. To him who overcomes, to him I will give some of the hidden manna, and I will give him a white stone, and a new name written on the stone which no one knows but he who receives it.* According to this verse what do you think it means to be one who "overcomes"?

4. Consider the Greek definition of "overcome" to the right and underline anything that gives you more insight into how God wants his people to live while on this Earth.

   Explain in your own words anything you find meaningful here:

WORD STUDY

Overcome: Greek *nikeõ* (Strong's G3528)

1) to conquer; to carry off the victory, come off victorious

2) of Christ, victorious over all his foes

3) of Christians, that hold fast their faith even unto death against the power of their foes, and temptations and persecutions

4) when one is arraigned or goes to law, to win the case, maintain one's cause.

5. In a university, passing a test is essential before you can move to the next level of classes. From James 1:2-4 in The Message Bible below, what role do tests and challenges have in our lives?

   2 *Consider it a sheer gift, friends, when tests and challenges come at you from all sides.*

   3 *You know that under pressure, your faith–life is forced into the open and shows its true colors.*

   4 *So don't try to get out of anything prematurely. Let it do its work so you become mature and well-developed, not deficient in any way.*

6. How could consistently practicing Deuteronomy 6:6-12 (see page 19) help you in the midst of your trials to overcome your flesh (the way you might be tempted to respond) and instead trust God to get you through?

7. How is being an over-comer a reflection of your growth? See James 1:2-4 if you need help.

Something to Think About:

The goal of this university is Christ-likeness in all tests, trials and tragedies. In order to grow and mature in Christ we must learn to overcome the impulses and desires of the flesh. Our flesh represents our sin nature. Its desires are completely opposite of God's Spirit within us (Gal. 5:17). Our sin nature compels us to seek comfort and provision in what the world offers instead of turning to God. In life we have two choices; to become a victim and be overcome by our circumstances or a victor and overcome our circumstances.

Wrapping it Up:

Life is a classroom. God wants to teach us to trust him and infuse his character into us every day. The key to learning to trust God is to know God. In Judges 2:10 we read that the people, *did not know the LORD, nor yet the work which He had done for Israel.* The Hebrew word for "know" is *yada* and it means "to understand, to grasp or ascertain; especially to be familiar or acquainted with a person or thing."* This doesn't mean knowledge about something or someone; instead it means to know by experience. It's a personal relationship. Only in relationship with God do we find the comfort and confidence we need to stand firm in the midst of our trials and troubles. Jesus said, *I have told you all this so that you may have peace in me. Here on earth you will have many trials and sorrows. But take heart, because I have overcome the world* (John 16:33 NLT).

Consider thinking through the following questions in your prayer time with the Lord.

1. Peace and trust are built in relationship with God. So how would you describe your relationship with him? Is it distant or growing in intimacy?

---

* Myers, A. C. (1987). *The Eerdmans Bible Dictionary* (880). Grand Rapids, Mich.: Eerdmans.

2. Are you learning to trust him more with each new trial or trouble? Explain your answer.

3. How can you consistently look to him and his strength to help you?

Application for Review

1. What is the most important lesson you have learned from Ruth 1:1–5?

2. What does it look like for us to depend on God in our trials and troubles?

3. If you can you relate or identify with any of the troubles that Elimelech and Naomi experienced, write your thoughts here.

4. Briefly review your study for this week. Try to identify any timeless principles you see in the character of the people or lessons from events or circumstances that might be considered relevant to our culture today. Record your thoughts here.

5. Spend some time in prayer; ask God what you can apply to your life from this lesson. If possible, write down one next step or a change you can make to align your life with God's desires for you.

Study Group Questions

1. Discuss the spiritual condition of the people in Ruth 1:1–5.

2. What do you think motivated Elimelech's decision to leave Bethlehem in Judah (i.e. fear, need, etc.)?

3. How can you consistently practice the principles identified Deuteronomy in 6:6–12? What steps can you take to make this a reality daily?

4. How can remembering the deeds of the Lord help you grow to know him more intimately?

5. Read James 1:2–4 on page 22. Discuss the purpose of trials in our lives. What are those trials designed to produce in our lives?

NOTES

I went out full,
but the Lord
has brought me
back empty.

—Ruth 1:21

LESSON THREE:

Emptied to be Filled

Life happens. At least that is how the saying goes. Life is a series of realities—some good and some bad. Jesus warned us that in this world we would have trouble. But how we *take*, or react to, the tests, trials, troubles, and tragedies reveals what is in our heart and who we are.

In the last lesson we met Elimelech, his wife Naomi, and their two sons Mahlon and Chilion. They left the Promised Land to live in the region of Moab to escape the famine in Bethlehem of Judah. They planned to sojourn there (stay temporarily), but instead remained. Not long after entering Moab, Elimelech died. Instead of returning to Bethlehem, Naomi and her sons remained and the sons took Moabite women as wives. Then, in what seems like the worst twist of fate, both of her sons died leaving behind their wives and their broken-hearted mother. Ruth 1:5 describes the scene this way: *then both Mahlon and Chilion also died, and the woman was bereft of her two children and her husband.* Hers was a life of shattered dreams. In this lesson we are going to explore the way Naomi reacted to the events of her life.

It is important to start this lesson with an attitude of humility and openness before God. Before we begin, pray our theme verse for this lesson.

Search me, O God, and know my heart; test me and know my anxious thoughts.
See if there is any offensive way in me, and lead me in the way everlasting. Psalm 139:23-24 (NIV)

Assignment One

While Naomi does a few things well, she was not consistent in her responses to her trials. Our goal is to become consistent over-comers.

Read Ruth 1:6–13 either in your Bible or in the *Appendix*. Write down what you observe. We've given you some hints below.

Observation of Ruth 1:6–13

1. Did you notice any repeated words in this passage? If so, list them below.

2. Where did Naomi decide to go and why?

3. What did she encourage her daughters-in-law to do? In the space below, note what she said.

4. What do you think motivated Naomi to urge her daughters-in-law to return?

5. What, if any, inconsistencies do you see in Naomi's behavior?

Two things Naomi did that are noteworthy:

1. She decided to return to Bethlehem in Judah.

   - Review what you learned about the meaning of the word "return" on pages 5 and 6, and read the Word Study box here. Based on what you learned, what does Ruth 1:6–13 imply about Naomi's decision to return to the land of Judah?

WORD STUDY

Return: To return is to turn back. In Hebrew this word is associated with repentance, but in the full sense of the word it is used to describe a complete change of orientation involving a judgment upon the past and a deliberate redirection for the future.*

---

* Myers, A. C. (1987). The *Eerdmans Bible Dictionary* (880). Grand Rapids, Mich.: Eerdmans.

   - What do you think caused Naomi to return to Bethlehem? Was it the need for food or could it be that hearing of the Lord's deliverance she realized that she was not living in the Promised Land given to them by God, but in the land of Moab outside his best for her? Record your thoughts below.

   - Considering the personal tragedies that Naomi experienced, how can losses like these in our own lives influence our decisions? (Consider personal tragedies like the death of dreams, relationships, loved ones and friendships, divorce, separation from significant people or places, etc.) How could these types of experiences affect your relationship with God?

2.   The second thing Naomi did well is she prayed for her daughters-in-law.

    •   Read again Ruth 1:9. What are the implications of Naomi's prayer for her daughters-in-law to find rest in the house of another husband?

    •   What do we learn from Naomi's prayer in Ruth 1:8-9 about her relationship with her daughters-in-law?

Something to Think About:

Sometimes our troubles cause us to realize that our choices have led us to become more self-reliant than God-reliant. We've slowly turned away from trusting in God. The turning is not always an abrupt change, but a slow, subtle turning away. Gradually we find ourselves taking comfort and satisfaction from things outside of God's best for us as Elimelech and his family did. This comfort and satisfaction can lead to complacency and complacency leads to compromise. Complacency is self-satisfaction accompanied by an unawareness of actual dangers or deficiencies. Remember, the family's original intent was a temporary stay in Moab. Instead they remained there, outside the Promise Land, and outside of God's best for them. I believe they slowly slipped further and further away from God because they chose to remain instead of return. Surrounded by Moabites who worshipped idols, the temptation would be to slowly slip away from living a God-dependant life. When we get complacent and comfortable we see no reason to take a good, hard look at our heart toward God and the things of God.

Assignment Two

In *Assignment One* we examined the two things Naomi did that were admirable. First she returned. She came to the end of herself and realized she needed to turn from Moab and return to her own people in the Promised Land. It is often difficult for us to admit our mistakes. Second she prayed for and expressed compassion for her daughters-in-law. It can be very difficult to pray for others when we are hurting. Today we'll take a closer look at Naomi's actions and what they reveal about her heart.

The Hebrew word for "heart" means the seat of moral character, the inner man. The heart is our genuine self. It is who we are when no one is looking. The condition of our heart is very important to God because it reveals our true unmasked character. Jesus said in Matthew 12:34, *For the mouth speaks out of that which fills the heart.* If we want to know the character issues we need to work on, we only need to listen to the words that come out of our mouths; if we pay attention to our words we can learn a lot about what is going on inside of us.

Read the following verses:

12 *Return, my daughters! Go, for I am too old to have a husband. If I said I have hope, if I should even have a husband tonight and also bear sons,*

13 *would you therefore wait until they were grown? Would you therefore refrain from marrying? No, my daughters; for it is harder for me than for you, for the hand of the LORD has gone forth against me.* Ruth 1:12–13

1. According to verse 12, what did Naomi lack?

2. What did Naomi say about her situation in verse 13?

3. From the worldly perspective, what facts made it hard for Naomi to have hope?

4. Where do you think Naomi was putting her hope?

Hope is defined as desire accompanied by expectation of or belief in fulfillment. The first characteristic we see in Naomi is _____lessness.

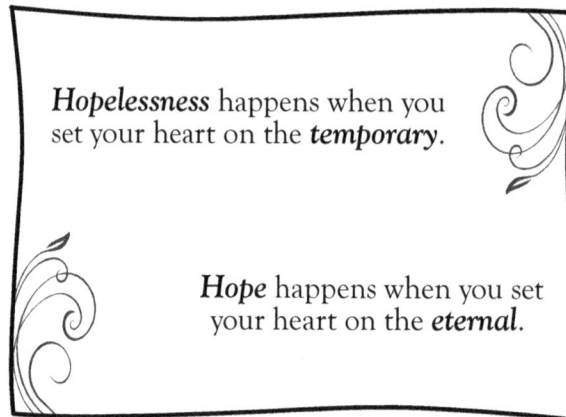

> *Hopelessness* happens when you set your heart on the *temporary*.
>
> *Hope* happens when you set your heart on the *eternal*.

Read 2 Corinthians 4:16–18:

16 *That is why we never give up. Though our bodies are dying, our spirits are being renewed every day.*

17 *For our present troubles are small and won't last very long. Yet they produce for us a glory that vastly outweighs them and will last forever!*

18 *So we don't look at the troubles we can see now; rather, we fix our gaze on things that cannot be seen. For the things we see now will soon be gone, but the things we cannot see will last forever.* (NLT)

In Scripture, hope is related to belief in God. Ephesians 2:12 says,

12 *In those days you were living apart from Christ. You were excluded from citizenship among the people of Israel, and **you did not know** the covenant promises God had made to them. You lived in this world **without** God and **without** hope.* (NLT)

Remember Naomi lived in the times of the judges when people did not _____ God (Judges 2:10).

5. What connection do you think there is between knowing God and having hope?

> *Let all that I am*
> *wait quietly before*
> *God, for my*
> *hope is in him.*
> Psalm 62:5

In the flesh we can't always see a way out of our circumstances. The question is: "Where are we looking?" Are we looking out *or up*? One of the greatest tests in life will be to *...fix our eyes on Jesus, the author and perfecter of our faith* (Heb. 12:2 NIV), despite our circumstances.

6. Let's look at the second characteristic lurking in Naomi's heart. Read the following verses:

> 12 *"Return, my daughters! Go, for I am too old to have a husband. If I said I have hope, if I should even have a husband tonight and also bear sons..."*
>
> 15 *Then she said, "Behold, your sister-in-law has gone back to her people and her gods; return after your sister-in-law." Ruth 1:12, 15*

What did Naomi encourage Ruth and Orpah to do? What word does she use?

7. By encouraging her daughters-in-law to return, what was she in effect sending them back to? See verse 15 for help.

8. Based on what you learned about Moabites in *Lesson One: Assignment One*, why do you think Naomi tried to send them back?

9. What do her actions reveal about her character?

The second characteristic lurking in Naomi's heart was <u>faithlessness</u>. When we fail to remember God's work in the past or if we don't know God, it is difficult to trust him. Trust is faith. It's difficult to trust someone you don't know.

Something to Think About:

I have to wonder what was in Naomi's heart that would cause her to encourage her daughters-in-law to return to their people and their gods. The Moabites were idol worshippers. One of the gods they worshipped was Chemosh. The sacrifice of children was part of the worship to this god! Could it be that Naomi wasn't thinking of this and the implications of it? Could it be that she did not want anyone in Bethlehem to know that her sons had taken Moabite women as wives? Could it be that as they started out she realized these Moabite women she loved would not be able to find husbands or even be accepted in Judah (Deut. 23:6; 1 Kings 11:1–2)? Could it be that Naomi was so overwhelmed by her circumstances (famine, moving from Bethlehem in Judah, the death of Elimelech and her two sons, and being destitute without support) that she was not only without hope, but bankrupt of faith in the goodness of God? Could it be she was mad at God? When people are mad at God it is often because he is not acting the way they think he should. In short, he is not living up to their expectations. Hopelessness combined with faithlessness leads to the last characteristic we see lurking in Naomi's heart. We'll explore that in our next assignment.

Assignment Three

In *Assignment Two* we began to explore what Naomi's words revealed about the condition of her heart. We learned that she was experiencing hopelessness and faithlessness. With everything that had happened in her life it's not surprising. It is entirely probable that she was disappointed with the way her life had turned out. Can you relate to her experiences? Have you ever found yourself angry at or disappointed with God? We must be on guard against our feelings. Feelings are not facts. While we may feel that God is not working on our behalf, or that he doesn't care about what is happening, that is simply not true. In fact in Psalm 139:16 we read:

16 *You saw me before I was born. Every day of my life was recorded in your book. Every moment was laid out before a single day had passed.* (NLT)

This means that God saw the good days as well as the bad days before we lived one of them. When we experience difficulties we must guard our hearts against feelings that contradict what we know is true about God. We must not let hopelessness and faithlessness take root in our hearts because it leads to the following characteristic we see in Naomi.

Guard your heart above all else, for it determines the course of your life.
Proverbs 4:23 (NLT)

1. Read Ruth 1:19-22:

19 *So they both went until they came to Bethlehem. And when they had come to Bethlehem, all the city was stirred because of them, and the women said, "Is this Naomi?"*

20 *She said to them, "Do not call me Naomi; call me Mara, for the Almighty has dealt very bitterly with me.*

21 *I went out full, but the LORD has brought me back empty. Why do you call me Naomi, since the LORD has witnessed against me and the Almighty has afflicted me?"*

22 *So Naomi returned, and with her Ruth the Moabitess, her daughter-in-law, who returned from the land of Moab. And they came to Bethlehem at the beginning of barley harvest.*

What question did the women in Bethlehem ask in verse 19? Why do you think they asked this question?

2.   What did Naomi want to be called?

3.   How did Naomi describe herself in verse 21?

4.   Who did she blame for her condition?

The final characteristic we see lurking in Naomi's heart is <u>bitterness</u>.

Did you notice Naomi, whose name means delightful, asked to be called Mara? Mara means bitter. Bitterness changes our countenance. Perhaps that is why the women in the town asked, *is this Naomi?* Bitterness makes us unrecognizable even to those who know us. Bitterness is destructive to believers. Its poison eats away at our heart until there is no room for loving others or for faith in God.

When you experience situations in your life that feel overwhelming and cause you to lose hope and doubt God, don't try to handle it alone. Instead, guard your heart by asking God for wisdom. James 1:2-5 says,

2   *Dear brothers and sisters, when troubles come your way, consider it an opportunity for great joy.*

3   *For you know that when your faith is tested, your endurance has a chance to grow.*

4   *So let it grow, for when your endurance is fully developed, you will be perfect and complete, needing nothing.*

5   *If you need wisdom, ask our generous God, and he will give it to you. He will not rebuke you for asking.* (NLT)

In the midst of trials and tests we can ask God for the wisdom we need to walk through the fire. God's wisdom will give us hope, strengthen our faith, and prevent bitterness. If we want to be consistent overcomers we must learn to pray and ask God for wisdom.

The final words of Naomi are perhaps the most powerful. Read Ruth 1:20-21 again.

5. What names does Naomi use for God?

6. What did Naomi say God had done to her?

7. What responsibility does she take, if any, for her own actions?

Bitterness will cause us to blame others for our situation. Bitterness blinds us to the work of God in our lives. In verse 21, Naomi blamed God for her circumstances although she called God by the name Almighty. In Hebrew the word Almighty is Shadday. It expresses God's sovereignty. In other words, the term expresses that God is in complete control at all times; both good and bad times are in his hands. Friends, you cannot have the sovereignty of God without the goodness of God. God's sovereignty will never contradict his character. First John 4:8 teaches us that *God is love*. His sovereignty will never violate his love. Even in the most difficult times of our lives God is still good and he is always love.

While on this Earth we will experience trials, tests, and troubles, we must learn that God always has our good in mind. Romans 8:28-29 says:

28 *And we know that God causes everything to work together for the good of those who love God and are called according to his purpose for them.*

29 *For God knew his people in advance, and he chose them to become like his Son, so that his Son would be the firstborn among many brothers and sisters.* (NLT)

Friends, a good God would not bring Naomi back empty and leave her that way. Sometimes the death of something—a dream, a relationship, a career—is the beginning of something new. God is all about new beginnings. It is no accident that Naomi returned to Bethlehem at the beginning of the harvest.

Something to Think About:

Can you think of situations in your life that, even though painful, God used for good? Look at the *Experience Tree.* On the trunk write a past situation or experience that was painful. On the branches write the good that has come from the test, trial or trouble. My beautiful friends, do not rush through this exercise. Instead, pray and ask God to show you the beauty in your heart and character that was birthed in the trial. Understand that in our difficulty God is working to bring life and hope to the places where there is pain and heartache.

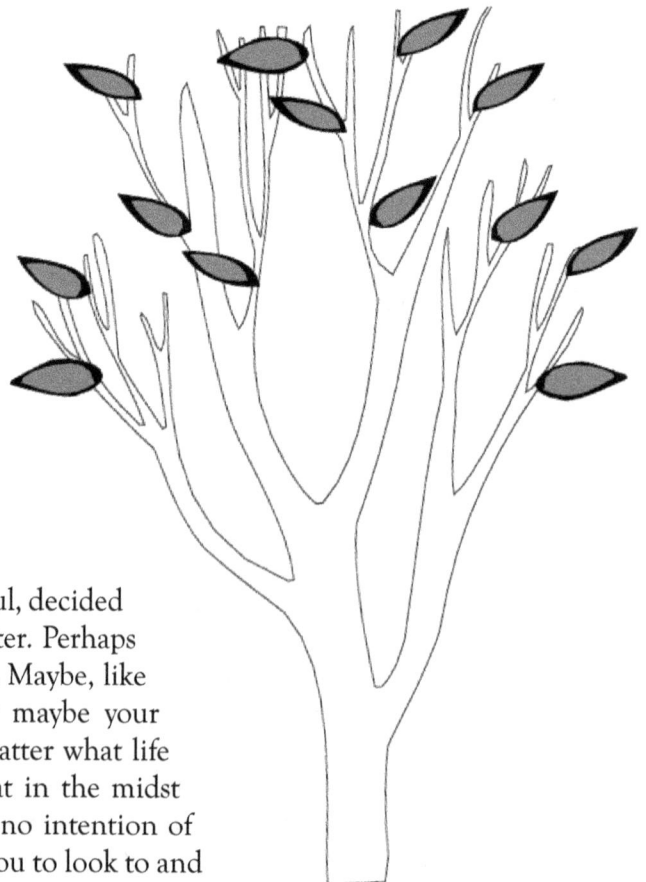

Wrapping it Up:

Life had become too much! Naomi, the delightful, decided she would rather be called Mara, the empty and bitter. Perhaps life has left you feeling overwhelmed and overcome. Maybe, like Naomi, your circumstances feel overwhelming or maybe your situation is more annoying than devastating. No matter what life may look like, it is important for you to know that in the midst of your test or trial God is there with you. He has no intention of leaving you alone to face the day. Instead, he wants you to look to and depend on him for the strength you need to thrive in every situation.

He wants us to maintain our hope, faith, and positive attitude while we endure life in the University of Refining Our Character. Most of all he wants to teach us about who he is through our trials and tests. He wants us to understand his character so we are able to trust him when times are tough. He wants us to remember that he is committed to working all things for the good of those who love him. He wants you to be unshaken by the curve balls of life. Beloved, he wants you to learn to say "God is good; all the time God is good!" ... and mean it.

Application for Review

1. When you have made a mistake, how difficult is it for you to admit it and repent? Elaborate on your answer.

2. What will it take for you to acknowledge responsibility for your mistakes? (Consider things like: truly knowing God personally, understanding his character, having assurance that he is trustworthy, discovering the joy of understanding his Word, realizing that God is love and he is always good, or one of your own.)

3. How do you *take* tests and trials? For example, do you blame God, praise God, or get mad at God? Do you crumble or stand faithfully?

4. How have you grown from your trials? If you haven't filled in your *Experience Tree*, commit to doing that by scheduling the time on your calendar.

5. Try to identify any timeless principles you see in the character of the people or lessons from events or circumstances that might be relevant to our culture today. Record your thoughts here.

6. Spend some time in prayer; ask God what you can apply to your life from this lesson. If possible, write down one next step or a change you can make to align your life with God's desires for you.

Study Group Questions

1. When we are faced with tests, trials, and tragedies, what might cause us to blame God?

2. Discuss how paying attention to what we say can help us recognize things we need to trust God to clean up in our lives.

3. Discuss the connection between knowing God and having hope. How does knowing him provide hope?

4. How has God used past trials to teach you more about who he is?

5. What is the most significant truth you learned in this lesson and why?

NOTES

LESSON FOUR:

Knowing God

In the last lesson we took a close look at Naomi. We explored her move from Bethlehem in the Promised Land to the territory belonging to Moab. We saw her interaction with her daughters-in-law and we watched her come to the end of herself as she passed through personal loss, hopelessness, and bitterness. In her own words, God emptied Naomi. But a good God would never empty her and leave her in that state; he emptied her so she could be filled. Her emptiness brought her to a place of surrender. Finally, she returned to her people in Bethlehem where she belonged. All Naomi's experiences were used by God to refine her character. God loves you just as you are, but he loves you too much to leave you as you are. Naomi is truly an example of this principle in action.

We have seen how failing to know the Lord or remembering all he has done for us can affect our reactions to life's tests, trials and tragedies. We learned that Naomi lived in a time when the people did not *know* the Lord or what he had done for Israel. We need to realize that trust begins in relationships. It's difficult to trust someone you do not know. The same is true of our relationship with God. Faith grows in relationship. As we get to know God by experience, we learn that God is good. His sovereignty will never violate his character. That means no matter what comes our way, he always has our best in mind, even when we can't see it and don't feel it.

With that in mind, this week we are going to dive deeper into God's character, his love, and, in particular, his sovereignty. Our prayer for you is *that the God of our Lord Jesus Christ, the glorious Father, may give you the Spirit of wisdom and revelation, so that you <u>may know him better</u>. I pray also that the eyes of your heart may be enlightened in order that you may know the hope to which he has called you, the riches of his glorious inheritance in the saints, and his incomparably great power for us who believe* (Eph. 1:17–19 NIV).

Assignment One

The earth is the Lord's, and all it contains, The world, and those who dwell in it.
Psalm 24:1

God is in Control

Why study the sovereignty of God? When Naomi returned to Bethlehem, she said, *"I went out full, but the Lord has brought me back empty. Why do you call me Naomi, since the Lord has witnessed against me and the Almighty has afflicted me?"* (Ruth 1:21).

Countless people blame God for the bad things that have happened in their lives, asking: "If God is good, then why did this happen to me?" While God allows tests and trials in our lives, we must never forget that through it all he is in complete control.

The Hebrew name for *Lord* that Naomi used in this passage is YHWH. His name is a frequent reminder that God's rule and authority rests ultimately upon his creation and ownership of all things and people.* While God is in complete control of the ultimate outcome, his actions will never violate his character. From time to time even mature believers struggle with the truth that God is sovereign and good at the same time. This is a very important lesson for us to learn—our time of growing spiritually and developing our character while we live on Earth.

How do we know God is in complete control of the ultimate outcome? We know because he tells the complete story. We have the beginning–Genesis, and we have the end–Revelation. Only someone outside the confines of time who controls everything could tell the entire story. God is the alpha, the omega, the beginning, and the end.

In this assignment we will study the meaning and implications of the sovereignty of God. Let's begin by gaining understanding of what exactly it means when we say that God is sovereign. Then we can look at what God's sovereignty meant in Naomi's life and what it means to us in the way we live our lives today.

WORD STUDY

Sovereign–noun
1. monarch; a king, queen, or other supreme ruler.
2. a person who has sovereign power or authority.
3. a group or body of persons or a state having sovereign authority.
–adjective
5. belonging to or characteristic of a sovereign or sovereignty; royal.
6. having supreme rank, power, or authority.
7. supreme; preeminent; indisputable: a sovereign right.
8. greatest in degree; utmost or extreme.
9. being above all others in character, importance, excellence, etc.

Adapted from http://dictionary.reference.com/browse/sovereign

---

* Elwell, W. A., & Beitzel, B. J. (1988). Baker Encyclopedia of the Bible (1346). Grand Rapids, Mich.: Baker Book House.

1. Read the English language definitions for sovereign in the Word Study box on page 46 to better understand what it means when we say that God is sovereign. After reading these definitions, write out in your own words why knowing that God is sovereign is important to help you understand who God is and his role in your life.

2. Ultimately God is in control of everything. In his sovereignty, God has a plan and purpose for all things that happen, even when we can't see the reasoning behind it all. How do Psalm 135:6 and Ephesians 1:11 below, help you to see that nothing is outside of God's control and perfect plan and purpose for us?

    11 *In him we were also chosen, having been predestined according to the plan of him who works out everything in conformity with the purpose of his will... Ephesians 1:11 (NIV)*

    6 *The Lord does whatever pleases him throughout all heaven and earth, and on the seas and in their depths. Psalm 135:6 (NLT)*

3. Read Proverbs 16:4, Ephesians 1:14, and John 16:33:

    4 *The Lord has made everything for his own purposes, even the wicked for a day of disaster. Proverbs 16:4 (NLT)*

    14 *The Spirit is God's guarantee that he will give us the inheritance he promised and that he has purchased us to be his own people. He did this so we would praise and glorify him. Ephesians 1:14 (NLT)*

    33 *I have told you these things, so that in me you may have peace. In this world you will have trouble. But take heart! I have overcome the world. John 16:33 (NIV)*

Is evil included in God's plans? How do you think God can be glorified while evil exists in this world?

One of the things that many people struggle with is the conflict in believing that God is good and perfect despite the bad things happening all around us. Take heart. You are not alone if you have difficulty reconciling these two truths. We all struggle to understand why God allows sin and evil to go on. We know from the Bible that God created us with genuine freedom—he gave each of us free will. Along with our ability to choose how we behave, we find we also do things that hurt others. The gift of free will that God gave to us is also the very thing that brings sin and evil into our world.

God is not the creator of evil, but in his sovereignty the free will he gave us has created evil. If God removed evil from the world he would have to remove our ability to choose what we do—we would be as robots. But ultimately God is in control and all evil will one day be judged by him and justice will be a reality for all his people in eternity. For now we live in a fallen world with the hope of eternity in God's presence where we will live in perfect peace and harmony.

4. God's sovereignty never lessens our free will, and free will never diminishes his sovereignty. What comfort does it give you to know that, even with our free will to choose, God is still sovereign?

5. How do you feel about Naomi's response toward God in Ruth 1:20-21?

20 *"Don't call me Naomi," she responded. "Instead, call me Mara, for the Almighty has made life very bitter for me.*

21 *I went away full, but the Lord has brought me home empty. Why call me Naomi when the Lord has caused me to suffer and the Almighty has sent such tragedy upon me?"* (NLT)

6. One of the most profound stories of suffering and loss in the Bible is the story of Job. In Job chapters 1 and 2, we read about all that happened to Job and his family. In one day Job lost all his wealth, his flocks, his servants, and finally all his children. In the midst of all of his adversity and loss, look at the way Job responded:

20 *Then Job arose and tore his robe and shaved his head, and he fell to the ground and worshiped.*

21 *He said,*

> *"Naked I came from my mother's womb,*
>
> *And naked I shall return there.*
>
> *The Lord gave and the Lord has taken away.*
>
> *Blessed be the name of the Lord."*

22 *Through all this Job did not sin nor did he blame God.* Job 1:20-22

Finally, Job lost his health when he was stricken with painful boils from head to toe. In frustration and anger his wife lashed out at his faith, but Job again responded with integrity. Read their exchange in Job 2:9-10:

9 *Then his wife said to him, "Do you still hold fast your integrity? Curse God and die!"*

10 *But he said to her, "You speak as one of the foolish women speaks. Shall we indeed accept good from God and not accept adversity?" In all this Job did not sin with his lips.*

- What does Job's response teach you about God's sovereignty?

- Based on Job's response to his trials what type of relationship do you think Job had with God?

7. Compare Naomi's response to her trial with Job's response to his trial. What differences do you see?

Something to Think About:

Like Job, Naomi lost much of her family and she was left with no means of support for herself and her daughters-in-law. Her life was not turning out as she expected. Naomi had legitimate losses that would leave most people feeling discouraged. In difficult and tragic times, finding a positive perspective and giving God worship as Job did is important.

Assignment Two

God is Good

God doesn't cause evil things to happen to you—that would make God evil. We know from the Bible that God is good and that God is love. In fact Exodus 34:6-7 describes God as *compassionate and gracious, slow to anger, and abounding in lovingkindness and truth; who keeps lovingkindness for thousands, who forgives iniquity, transgression and sin.* That doesn't sound like God is one who would cause bad things to happen to you does it? We need to know that his actions will never violate his sovereignty.

What makes God good? God's goodness is demonstrated in his actions toward us. Today we are going to explore God's goodness through the eyes of the Psalmist David.

1. Read Psalm 103:1-18. Circle every reference, either stated or implied, to God's goodness in this passage.

    1   Let all that I am praise the Lord; with my whole heart, I will praise his holy name.

    2   Let all that I am praise the Lord; may I never forget the good things he does for me.

    3   He forgives all my sins and heals all my diseases.

    4   He redeems me from death and crowns me with love and tender mercies.

    5   He fills my life with good things. My youth is renewed like the eagle's!

    6   The Lord gives righteousness and justice to all who are treated unfairly.

    7   He revealed his character to Moses and his deeds to the people of Israel.

    8   The Lord is compassionate and merciful, slow to get angry and filled with unfailing love.

    9   He will not constantly accuse us, nor remain angry forever.

    10 He does not punish us for all our sins; he does not deal harshly with us, as we deserve.

    11 For his unfailing love toward those who fear him is as great as the height of the heavens above the earth.

    12 He has removed our sins as far from us as the east is from the west.

    13 The Lord is like a father to his children, tender and compassionate to those who fear him.

14   For he knows how weak we are; he remembers we are only dust.

15   Our days on earth are like grass; like wildflowers, we bloom and die.

16   The wind blows, and we are gone—as though we had never been here.

17   But the love of the Lord remains forever with those who fear him. His salvation extends to the children's children

18   of those who are faithful to his covenant, of those who obey his commandments! (NLT)

• List the good things God has filled your life with despite your tests and trials.

• What can you do to help yourself remember to intentionally praise God regularly?

• How might enduring your trials be different if you remember his goodness toward you?

2.   Review the good things you circled in the Psalm. Which of these is the most significant to you and why?

What does it mean when the Bible describes the Lord as compassionate?

Psalm 103, verse eight, tells us that God is compassionate. When God calls himself compassionate as he did in Exodus 34:6, it is important that we understand what that means. *Merriam Webster Dictionary* defines compassion as: a sympathetic consciousness of others' distress together with a desire to alleviate it. While it is sometimes difficult to get a clear picture of God's compassion, synonyms help us to gain a better understanding. Synonyms for compassionate include: tender, kindhearted, responsive, softhearted, sympathetic, warm, warmhearted.

---

3. What does the boxed definition of compassionate and its synonyms, on the previous page, imply about how God feels toward you and the difficulties you experience?

4. From Psalm 103, what does verse 13 say the Lord is like? Describe the feelings this verse bring to mind.

5. According to Psalm 103:10, God does not do what? Fill in the blanks below.

   God does not _____ for all our sins; he does not deal _____ with us, as we deserve.

6. Remember Naomi's words in Ruth 1:21b: *Why call me Naomi when the Lord has caused me to suffer and the Almighty has sent such tragedy upon me* (NLT). Naomi felt like her suffering—her losses—were caused by God being harsh with her. What does Psalm 103:10 teach you about our tendency to see our tests and trials as punishment from God?

Something to Think About:

I grew up hearing "God is good, all the time. All the time God is good." I have learned that God is good despite my circumstances. Let's get real. There is a big difference between God allowing tests and trials in our lives and God causing them. I have also learned that often times when people cry out and declare that God has been harsh with them or even cruel, as in Naomi's case, it was because God did not act as they thought he should in their circumstance. God is good even when life is at its worst. He mourns with us when we mourn, he hurts when we hurt, but if he removed all the pain and suffering we experience, how would we ever come to depend upon and trust him? How would we grow in our relationship with him if life were always easy and comfortable? The biggest mistake we can ever make in life is to think that suffering, heartache, death, and cruelty are the work of God. They are not. They are the result of sin and living in a fallen world. However, at the center of all that happens in life is a completely loving, completely faithful, completely in control God. The question is—will you trust him? Will you trust him when life isn't good? Will you love him when all seems lost? Will you look for his goodness despite your pain?

Assignment Three

Where is God When Bad Things Happen?

We all feel perplexed at times by seeing bad things happening to good people. We are distressed when we see wicked people get ahead and good people struggle. Naomi didn't understand why her husband and sons died prematurely. She didn't know why she was left without a way to provide for herself and her daughters-in-law. But she did know to return to God's people in Bethlehem of Judah. There she found God to be more than adequate to provide for all her needs. In Job's story God never told him why he allowed him to suffer so much. Instead, God reminded Job of the immensity of his creative power and divine wisdom. In the end, Job felt foolish for having questioned God and humbly repented.

1. From what you know about Naomi and Job's losses, how important do you think it was for them to understand "why" they were struck with tragedy? Do you think they were satisfied with seeing God's blessing and provision as they looked back over their lives? Explain your answer.

2. Read Romans 8:28–29 below. How do you think trusting God in the midst of difficulties can benefit us today?

    28 *And we know that God causes everything to work together for the good of those who love God and are called according to his purpose for them.*

    29 *For God knew his people in advance, and he chose them to become like his Son, so that his Son would be the firstborn among many brothers and sisters.* (NLT)

3. Romans 8:28 tells us that if we are called by God according to his purpose for us, he will work all things together for good. How can we be certain that we are called according to God's purpose for us? Read 1 Peter 2:9 for help clarifying what it means to be called by God.

4. Read James 1:2–4. Write out what you learn about how and why God allows tests of our faith. How do you feel about the idea that God would allow circumstances that test your faith? How do verses 1 through 4 help you understand God's motives and purpose for these tests and trials?

5. Go back to Question 2 and reread Romans 8:28–29. How do these verses translate into the hope that you need for facing each day?

Something To Think About:

You know, it is easy to wonder why God allows us to face hardships and heartache. I personally take comfort in Romans 8:28-29. Paul never doubted God during those times; instead he stood on what he knew. He knew God could take the most hurtful, most disturbing, most challenging events of his life and somehow use the situation for his good. He knew that good would come from what he perceived as bad because he trusted in and had faith in God. What would it take for you to react with the same confidence and faith Paul had in tests and trials?

Wrapping It Up:

God is Good. All the time God is good! In this lesson we have explored the character of God. Being able to stand firm and not be overcome by our circumstances is rooted in our trust in a completely good, loving, and faithful God. Nahum 1:7 says, *The LORD is good, a refuge in times of trouble. He cares for those who trust in him...* (NIV). When you face trouble remember God is your refuge, your safe place. When life comes crashing down it is his arms that protect and hold you; his strength that will sustain you. He cares for you. One day he will wipe every tear from your eye. Until then, he wants you to know he loves you.

Study Group Questions

1. Discuss the importance of understanding the sovereignty of God.

2. Naomi verbalized her belief that God brought trouble into her life in Ruth 1:20-21. Why is it so easy for us to blame God when bad things happen? How can our faith in the goodness and love of God help us deal with trials and troubles with an appropriate perspective?

3. In Psalm 73:1-5 the psalmist said, *No doubt about it! God is good—good to good people, good to the good-hearted. But I nearly missed it, missed seeing his goodness. I was looking the other way* (The Message). Discuss some attitudes, habits, or lifestyle behaviors that could cause us to miss seeing God's goodness in our lives daily.

4. Read 1 Peter 5:7-9. How can recognizing that you have a spiritual enemy motivate you to be prepared to stand firm in your faith?

5. How do Romans 8:28-29 and Romans 8:38-39 help you see that God has given you all you need to have confidence in his strength when you face tests, trials and troubles?

NOTES

Now, my daughter, do not fear...for all my people...know that you are a woman of excellence.

—Ruth 3:11

Lesson Five:

A Woman of Excellence—Part One

The character God develops in us is the key component to becoming a consistent over-comer. Trusting and believing in God's goodness is the foundation upon which we build our character. Since the goal of UROC is Christ-like character, we must begin by understanding that his character, and therefore his actions toward us, flow from goodness and love despite what we experience in life.

In our last lesson, we caught up with Naomi after the loss of her husband and her two sons. In response to her tragedies, Naomi did some things right and some things wrong. Life became too much; the delightful Naomi chose to be called Mara, the empty and bitter. But a good God would not empty Naomi to leave her that way; he emptied her to fill her again with something better than she had before. God is interested in how we "take" our circumstances and trials; he uses difficulties to reveal our heart; he wants to change our hearts to be like his (Job 23:10). He wants to transform us into women of excellence. In this lesson we look at the way Ruth responded to the challenges and circumstances of her life. Her response displays six character traits of a consistent over-comer. This week we will examine three of those traits and how, when we respond in kind, we too can become women of excellence.

Assignment One

Faithful

How do you respond when tragedy and trouble come your way? While it is natural for us to experience feelings such as fear, sadness, frustration, and anger, how we act upon those feelings is a test of our character. In response to fear do we run and hide or do we boldly and courageously face the day? In the midst of sadness can we see past our pain and still hope? In frustration and anger do we lash out at others or do we hold our tongue and composure? The mark of a woman of excellence is that in the midst of life's challenges she does not give in to her feelings—she rises above them.

As we review the character qualities of a woman of excellence it is important to define them. Write your understanding of what it means to be faithful here.

The *Holman Bible Dictionary* defines faithful as steadfast, dedicated, dependable, and worthy of trust. Before you begin today's lesson, read Ruth 1. Look for the ways in which Ruth was faithful.

1. Read Ruth 1:15–18:

   15   *Then she said, "Behold, your sister-in-law has gone back⁷⁷²⁵ to her people and her gods; return⁷⁷²⁵ after your sister-in-law."*

   16   *But Ruth said, "Do not urge me to leave⁵⁸⁰⁰ you or turn back⁷⁷²⁵ from following you; for where you go¹⁹⁸⁰, I will go¹⁹⁸⁰, and where you lodge, I will lodge. Your people shall be my people, and your God, my God.*

   17   *Where you die, I will die, and there I will be buried. Thus may the LORD do to me, and worse, if anything but death parts you and me."*

   18   *When she saw that she was determined to go with her, she said no more to her.*

What was Ruth's response when Naomi urged her to turn back and return to her people? See verses 16–17. Record your thoughts here.

2. Read the definitions in the Word Studies box; then read Ruth 1:15–17 again, keeping any new insight in mind. Record any thoughts that seem important about Naomi and Ruth's conversation.

Record your thoughts here:

3. In verse 16, Ruth says, *Do not urge me to leave you or turn back from following you for where you go, I will go....* After reading the word study for the word "go," how does the definition change the way you understand the meaning of verse 16?

> **WORD STUDIES**
>
> **"leave"** – Strong's Exhaustive Concordance #5800 means to forsake or abandon
>
> **"turn"** – Strong's #7725 means "back" (It is the same Hebrew word that we see used in Ruth 1:15 for return. This word is used repeatedly in verses 15 and 16) It means to turn back—return
>
> **"go"** – Strong's #1980, according to Mounce's Expository Dictionary, describes motion, primarily of humans, and is usually translated "walk, go, come." It is also used in a metaphorical sense to describe actions or the process of living, especially following or walking in the ways of the LORD.

Considering Ruth's background, what makes her statement to Naomi so remarkable?

Who did Ruth declare her faith in?

4. Read Ruth 1:16–17 again. Use the chart below to record your ideas about Ruth's decisions or motives for each commitment she made to Naomi.

    Ruth's Statement   **Ruth's Decision or Motive**

    Example: Where you go I will go   Commitment to Naomi

5. How do you think Naomi felt as she saw the depth of Ruth's faithfulness?

    Think of a time in your life when you were able to remain faithful to God or to a friend. What choices did you make in order to remain faithful?

6. According to 1 John 5:4 below, what is the relationship between faith and overcoming the world?

    4   *For whatever is born of God overcomes the world; and this is the victory that has overcome the world—our faith.*

Something to Think About:

In her young life Ruth suffered many losses. She lost, through death, her father-in-law, her brother-in-law, and her husband. She was childless and a widow. She also experienced rejection when her mother-in-law began pushing her away. Ruth could have become bitter and returned to Moab, but she chose to stay with Naomi exercising patience, gentleness, and self-control. She chose to rise above her circumstances and chose faith over her feelings. She chose to have faith in God, and be faithful to her friend Naomi who was bitter and hopeless. Ruth made a choice. In the midst of life's difficulties we too can choose to be faithful and, in doing so, not only will we be victorious overcomers, we will also become more Christ-like. What type of character do you want to display in the midst of life's difficulties; Naomi's or Ruth's?

Assignment Two

Loyalty

When we are faithful to others, it is known as loyalty. When it comes to loyalty nothing expresses the depth and beauty of it quite like God's Covenant. A covenant is a promise between two parties cut by the sacrificial shedding of blood which binds them together. Not even death broke the bonds of loyalty between covenant parties because their descendants benefited from the covenant relationship. The two parties would utilize covenant language and call down upon themselves the same fate that befell the animals should anything but death separate them. In Genesis, God made an everlasting covenant with Abram and his descendants. That Covenant is rich with meaning and the words used in Genesis 15 are recognized as "covenant language." The Hebrew people of Ruth's day and the Jewish people throughout history unto this day recognize the significance hidden within the covenant language. Generations of Israelites would pass down the story of how God promised to protect and bless his children. Naomi, her husband, and sons, were beneficiaries of the Covenant. Even though they lived in a time when people did not know the Lord, it is likely that because they lived in the Promised Land, they knew of God's covenant with Israel.

Write your understanding of what it means to be loyal here:

Read Ruth 1:14–18. Look for the ways Ruth demonstrated loyalty to Naomi.

1. In Ruth 1:17, Ruth said to Naomi: *Where you die, I will die, and there I will be buried. Thus may the LORD do to me, and worse, if anything but death parts you and me.* Although we do not see Ruth cutting a covenant in blood with Naomi, we do hear Ruth use covenant language—her promise that only death would separate them. Ruth took her commitment to Naomi as seriously as if it was a walk unto death. What does Ruth's "unto death" commitment and loyalty to Naomi reveal about their relationship?

2. Keeping in mind that Ruth was a Moabite and was not included in the Covenant that God made with Israel (Gen. 15), her knowledge of covenant had to be learned; but how?

3. Ruth knew Naomi well enough to see that she was in a bad place spiritually. Naomi was empty but Ruth was committed to providing for her needs. How is their relationship a demonstration of Ecclesiastes 4:9–10 below?

    9 *Two people are better off than one, for they can help each other succeed.*

    10 *If one person falls, the other can reach out and help. But someone who falls alone is in real trouble.* (NLT)

4. What role have Godly women played in your life? Below write a thank you note to a spiritual sister who has stood by you during a difficult time. If possible thank her in person. If you do not have a close friend pray and ask God to send you a loyal friend like Ruth.

5. Look up the following verses and note the weaknesses we struggle with. Write your thoughts next to the verse references.

   • Ecclesiastes 4:9-12

   • Hebrews 3:13-14

   • Jeremiah 17:9

   • Exodus 17:8-13

   Considering the weaknesses we have, how do you think having a friend or accountability partner can strengthen and encourage us when we need someone to have our back?

6. What are some ways you can demonstrate loyalty in your relationships?

Something to Think About:

Ruth was loyal to Naomi and that loyalty was slowly breaking down the walls that surrounded Naomi. Ruth remained faithful and loyal while Orpah turned back as Naomi had encouraged her to do. The last few years of my life have really illustrated just how important it is to have a friend who has my back—one who won't walk out on me when life gets hard—a wingman. I spent many years not being able to get along with women. My own personal jealousies and petty insecurities kept me from having meaningful transparent relationships with women in my life. However, in my late thirties the Lord began to work in my heart to break the bondage of low self-esteem. As the walls of insecurity came crashing down, God surrounded me with women who loved me as I was—messy. They made me feel safe and accepted. Those women began to speak into my life, encouraging me to grow, helping me to stand in my faith, and challenging me as iron sharpens iron. They have walked with me through life's ups and downs. I know I would not be the woman I am today without them. They are irreplaceable treasure in my life. My relationship with the Lord is stronger because they have modeled the faith that I wanted. When I was frightened by the loss of job security, cancer, child rearing challenges, and leadership ups and downs, they were there to pray and lend their support. When we are loyal to our friends we are demonstrating Christ-like character because he promised, *never will I leave you or forsake you* (Heb. 13:5 NRSV).

Assignment Three

Determined

Naomi tried to convince Ruth to return to Moab, to her former way of life, and to the Moabite gods. But, we see Ruth stand her ground in steadfast determination in Ruth 1:16–17. She was not willing to return. She would not go back to her former way of life nor would she abandon her friend. Instead she resolved to press on to a new life with new possibilities.

Write below your understanding of what it means to be determined.

> **WORD STUDY**
>
> To be *determined* is the act of deciding definitely and being firm in purpose and resolve. In the Bible the original Hebrew word adds this insight to the definition: to be determined, to make oneself alert, strengthen oneself, confirm oneself, persist in, prove superior to.*
>
> _____
>
> * Strong, J. (1996). The exhaustive concordance of the Bible: Showing every word of the text of the common English version of the canonical books, and every occurrence of each word in regular order. (electronic ed.). Ontario: Woodside Bible Fellowship.

1. Read Ruth 1:14-18 and 2:1-7 and record examples of Ruth's determination in the space below.

Ruth showed strength in her choices. She was determined to overcome her pain and embrace a better life. She wanted something more than brokenness. Her determination to do what was right benefited Naomi and changed the course of both their lives. Let's look at another example of the benefits of determination in Scripture.

2. Read Mark 2:1-12:

   1 *When He had come back to Capernaum several days afterward, it was heard that He was at home.*

   2 *And many were gathered together, so that there was no longer room, not even near the door; and He was speaking the word to them.*

   3 *And they came, bringing to Him a paralytic, carried by four men.*

   4 *Being unable to get to Him because of the crowd, they removed the roof above Him; and when they had dug an opening, they let down the pallet on which the paralytic was lying.*

   5 *And Jesus seeing their faith said to the paralytic, "Son, your sins are forgiven."*

   6 *But some of the scribes were sitting there and reasoning in their hearts,*

   7 *"Why does this man speak that way? He is blaspheming; who can forgive sins but God alone?"*

   8 *Immediately Jesus, aware in His spirit that they were reasoning that way within themselves, said to them, "Why are you reasoning about these things in your hearts?*

   9 *Which is easier, to say to the paralytic, 'Your sins are forgiven'; or to say, 'Get up, and pick up your pallet and walk'?*

   10 *But so that you may know that the Son of Man has authority on earth to forgive sins"—He said to the paralytic,*

   11 *"I say to you, get up, pick up your pallet and go home."*

   12 *And he got up and immediately picked up the pallet and went out in the sight of everyone, so that they were all amazed and were glorifying God, saying, "We have never seen anything like this."*

What were the four men who carried the paralytic determined to do? What obstacles did they face?

3. What was the result of their determination to bring their friend to Jesus?

4. What similarities do you see in Ruth and the four men?

5. What are you are determined to overcome? How can your determination influence or benefit others?

6. How does our determination to overcome bring glory to God?

Something to Think About:

Both Ruth and the four friends of the paralytic were determined to accomplish a task that brought about life-changing results. In Ruth's case, her commitment to overcome her tragic circumstances changed the course of both hers and Naomi's lives. The determination of the four friends of the paralytic not only brought about the opportunity for the man to be healed, but all present at the time glorified God (Mark 2:1–12). Jesus was also determined. The night before he was crucified he prayed, *"Abba, Father,"..."everything is possible for you. Please take this cup of suffering away from me. Yet I want your will to be done, not mine"* (Mark 14:36 NLT). He was determined to do the will of his father, and his determination benefited all of us. Determination is a Christ-like character quality.

Wrapping it Up:

I believe we often underestimate the influence we have in the lives of others. But it is clear both from Ruth and the story of the paralytic that we have been given a tremendous opportunity to be used by God to influence and affect the lives of other people for the better. God wants to use the character he is building in us to help others overcome their difficulties and challenges. He wants to use us to be there for others in their tests and trials and to remain faithful for those whose faith is failing. One thing is certain, we were not meant to live as lone rangers. We need each other. I can benefit from your strength of character and you can benefit from mine. The challenge is to push past our fears and be willing and open to be in relationship with others.

Practical Exercise

1. Are you currently experiencing a trial or a test? If not, think of a time of testing or trial from your recent past. Briefly describe it in the space below.

2. From this lesson, review the first three character traits of a woman of excellence. As you think about the circumstance you described above, how could practicing one of these traits bring glory to God and help you overcome the situation?

3. What can you do this week to put into practice one of the characteristics of a woman of excellence as you seek to overcome your circumstance?

4. If you have not made a decision to firmly press on, ask God to help you be determined to overcome.

Study Group Questions

1. From your study of Ruth 1:15-17, what strikes you as significant about Ruth's refusal to return to Moab when Naomi encouraged her to do so?

2. What character traits do you see in Ruth that could cause others to believe that Ruth was truly a woman of excellence?

3. Why do you think being of "faithful" character is valuable in our relationships with others and with God?

> **Faithful** has a variety of meanings. Look it up in the dictionary for further insight.

4. From your study in *Assignment Two* how is Ruth's loyalty to Naomi similar to God's loyalty to his people, as he clearly demonstrated through the Covenant he made with his people in Genesis 15?

5. Considering our human weaknesses, how do the verses you looked up in *Assignment Two*, question 5, reveal our need for a loyal friend or accountability partner to strengthen and encourage us when we need someone to have our back?

6. Depending on circumstances the character trait of "determination" could be viewed as either positive or negative. Discuss some ways that "determination" can be a valuable trait in a friend and from God's perspective.

7. In *Assignment One* we looked at the determination of Ruth to remain with Naomi and see to her needs. We also saw four men overcome obstacles that resulted in the healing of a paralyzed man. What are some practical everyday situations when determination can show us to be women of excellence?

NOTES

LESSON SIX:

A Woman of Excellence—Part Two

Becoming a woman of excellence requires that we consistently demonstrate godly character qualities in the midst of life's tests, trials and triumphs. Last week we learned that faithfulness, loyalty, and determination characterized Ruth's response to her personal tragedy. In this lesson we continue to look at what caused people around Ruth to recognize her as a woman of excellence.

As we continue our study we need to remember that the history of the relationship between Moab and Israel was tumultuous. Moabites were considered outcasts and enemies of Israel and were excluded from the Covenant that God made with Israel (Gen. 15). Ruth's knowledge of the Covenant was likely learned from Naomi. For a young woman, Ruth suffered many losses including the deaths of her father-in-law, her brother-in-law, and her husband. Ruth showed strength of character in her choices. She was determined to overcome her pain and embrace a better life. Ruth's determination to live right in God's eyes benefited Naomi and changed the course of their lives.

Assignment One

Courageous

In our last lesson we saw Ruth take a courageous stand against Naomi's urging her to return to Moab. In Ruth 1:16–17 she spoke to Naomi with fearless courage and declared:

16   "Do not urge me to leave you or turn back from following you; for where you go, I will go, and where you lodge, I will lodge. Your people shall be my people, and your God, my God.

17   Where you die, I will die, and there I will be buried. Thus may the LORD do to me, and worse, if anything but death parts you and me."

Ruth had no idea what her life would be like. She knew that Moab and Israel had a tumultuous history and trust between the nations was weak at best; she could easily face opposition in Naomi's community. Yet she willingly left the comfort of the land she knew and journeyed to an unfamiliar land where the people might not accept her. Ruth could have chosen comfort, friends, and her own family, but instead she courageously embraced a new life with an uncertain future.

Write your understanding of what it means to be courageous here.

Before beginning your lesson today read all of Ruth chapter two.

1. Considering what you know about Ruth and her background, why do you think going to Bethlehem with Naomi was more attractive than returning to her gods and her people?

2. What might you have done if you were Ruth?

3. Read Ruth 2:1-6:

> 1   Now Naomi had a kinsman of her husband, a man of great wealth, of the family of Elimelech, whose name was Boaz.
>
> 2   And Ruth the Moabitess said to Naomi, "Please let me go to the field and glean among the ears of grain after one in whose sight I may find favor." And she said to her, "Go, my daughter."
>
> 3   So she departed and went and gleaned in the field after the reapers; and she happened to come to the portion of the field belonging to Boaz, who was of the family of Elimelech.
>
> 4   Now behold, Boaz came from Bethlehem and said to the reapers, "May the LORD be with you." And they said to him, "May the LORD bless you."
>
> 5   Then Boaz said to his servant who was in charge of the reapers, "Whose young woman is this?"
>
> 6   The servant in charge of the reapers replied, "She is the young Moabite woman who returned with Naomi from the land of Moab."

From what you know about Ruth at this point, why do you think it might have taken courage for Ruth to go to the fields to glean? See verses 2 and 3 to see what Ruth committed to doing.

4. What further insight does Ruth 2:8-9 below give you regarding what could happen to a young woman in the fields?

> 8   Then Boaz said to Ruth, "Listen carefully, my daughter. Do not go to glean in another field; furthermore, do not go on from this one, but stay here with my maids.
>
> 9   Let your eyes be on the field which they reap, and go after them. Indeed, I have commanded the servants not to touch you. When you are thirsty, go to the water jars and drink from what the servants draw."

5.   How did courage help Ruth overcome the obstacles to a better life in Bethlehem?

6.   Joshua led the Israelites into the Promised Land where Ruth and Naomi now lived in Bethlehem of Judah. Read Moses' account of God calling Joshua in Deuteronomy 31:7–8. What role do you think courage played as Joshua answered God's call to lead the Israelites into the Promised Land?

> 7   *Then Moses called for Joshua, and as all Israel watched, he said to him, "Be strong and courageous! For you will lead these people into the land that the LORD swore to their ancestors he would give them. You are the one who will divide it among them as their grants of land.*
>
> 8   *Do not be afraid or discouraged, for the LORD will personally go ahead of you. He will be with you; he will neither fail you nor abandon you." (NLT)*

7.   Which promises do you think gave Joshua comfort and courage?

8.   Second Timothy 1:7 says:

> 7   *For God has not given us a spirit of timidity, but of power and love and discipline.*

Courage and faith go together. It took faith and courage for Joshua to answer God's call. It took courage for Ruth to go to Bethlehem and for her to glean in the fields instead of returning to Moab.

In what area of your life do you need courage?

Something to Think About:

Fear is the great enemy of faith. When we are fearful we will not act in power, love or discipline. Instead, fear causes side effects such as control issues, anger, and irrational thoughts. Instead of overcoming in our tests and trials, fear can cause us to be overwhelmed by them. Fear can keep us from experiencing God's best for us. Over and over in Scripture God encourages us by saying, *do not fear*, or *be strong and courageous*. While these words are encouraging, many of us suffer from fear and its effects.

Recently, I had one of the most fearful experiences of my life. It was time for my annual mammogram. The parting words of the technician were "we will only call you if it is something bad." The phone rang at 4:55 on Friday afternoon. The message was simply get back in right away. Of course, I didn't retrieve the message until long after the office was closed for the weekend. For the next two days I was overwhelmed with the fear of "what if."

In my agony I cried out to God and he gave me the same Scripture you studied today in Deuteronomy 31:8. I clung to that verse over the weekend and as I sat in the office awaiting the results. As I left that day I handed that Scripture verse, which I had written on a piece of paper, to the woman who sat next to me, also waiting for the results of her third test. "This has comforted me, I pray it comforts you" was all I said. The tears in her eyes told me all I needed to know.

The truth is we all experience feelings of fear, but in the midst of our trials we cannot let our feelings overrun our thoughts or determine our reactions. We must courageously cling to the truth and our confidence in God's love for us. Christ was courageous as he faced his greatest trial—the cross. A person with Christ-like character courageously faces life's tests, trials and tragedies because they trust in God's plan for their life despite what they see and feel. The way to overcome fear is to meditate on, claim, and recite Scriptures. See *Be Courageous* and *Overcoming Fear* in the *Appendix* for verses to encourage you to be courageous no matter the situation you are facing.

Assignment Two

Humble

True humility is a beautiful quality that seems so difficult to define and find today. Many of us who think we are humble are more likely suffering from self-abasement, which means we degrade or humiliate ourselves because of feelings of guilt or because we feel inferior. True humility comes from a very real understanding of who God is and who he created us to be. A truly humble person doesn't spend much time thinking about their own needs but is more content with thoughts of God and meeting the needs others. This person doesn't need to downplay herself, nor does she have the need to elevate herself. She is content with the way God created her and her great joy is in living out his purposes for her life.

Write your understanding of what it means to be humble here.

1. Read Ruth 2:8–10 below, keeping in mind that the culture of Boaz's day was very different from the one we live in today. From what you know about Ruth and the culture of that day, why do you think Ruth prostrated herself before Boaz?

    8   *Then Boaz said to Ruth, "Listen carefully, my daughter. Do not go to glean in another field; furthermore, do not go on from this one, but stay here with my maids.*

    9   *Let your eyes be on the field which they reap, and go after them. Indeed, I have commanded the servants not to touch you. When you are thirsty, go to the water jars and drink from what the servants draw."*

    10 *Then she fell on her face, bowing to the ground and said to him, "Why have I found favor in your sight that you should take notice of me, since I am a foreigner?"*

2. Humility is hard for us to understand—it requires us to recognize our position before God. But false humility can be nothing more than pride demanding that others acknowledge something about us that isn't evident. How can we be sure that humility is genuine and not pride at work in us? Consider the verses below to gain understanding about true humility. Record your thoughts in the chart below.

    "My hands have made both heaven and earth; they and everything in them are mine." I, the LORD, have spoken! "I will bless those who have humble and contrite hearts, who tremble at my word." Isaiah 66:2 (NLT)

    For those who exalt themselves will be humbled, and those who humble themselves will be exalted." Luke 14:11 (NLT)

    Pride ends in humiliation, while humility brings honor. Proverbs 29:23 (NLT)

    Remind the people to be subject to rulers and authorities, to be obedient, to be ready to do whatever is good, to slander no one, to be peaceable and considerate, and to show true humility toward all men. Titus 3:1-2 (NIV)

WHAT ARE THE RESULTS OF PRIDE?	WHAT ARE THE RESULTS OF HUMILITY?

3. Ruth did not think more highly of herself than she ought to. In fact, she considered Naomi's needs more important than her own. She is an example of Philippians 2:3-4 in action. What would it look like for you to practice this passage daily?

   3   *Do nothing out of selfish ambition or vain conceit, but in humility consider others better than yourselves.*

   4   *Each of you should look not only to your own interests, but also to the interests of others.* (NIV)

4. From Ruth 2:17-18, in what ways do you see Ruth providing for Naomi? How is this a demonstration of Philippians 2:3-4?

   17   *So she gleaned in the field until evening. Then she beat out what she had gleaned, and it was about an ephah of barley.*

   18   *She took it up and went into the city, and her mother-in-law saw what she had gleaned. She also took it out and gave Naomi what she had left after she was satisfied.*

5. In her circumstances Naomi would have had a difficult time providing for herself. Her age and her emotional condition after the death of her family were working against her strength and possibly her will to live. Ruth's care for Naomi when she was most vulnerable was critical to her survival. What lessons do you learn from Ruth's care for Naomi?

6. From Ruth's example, humility and selflessness go hand in hand. In your opinion how are these qualities Christ-like?

Something to Think About:

We will all experience times of great spiritual, emotional and physical hardship. I can recall a time when my emotional strength was failing me. I had been through a very difficult year of ministry and as a result I wanted to give up. I told my closest friends that because of the personal criticisms and the fact that God wasn't showing up, at least not the way I wanted him to, I was going to quit and move on to a new phase of my life. Well, my friends rallied around me, one in particular, Linda, came alongside me and refused to let me quit. She challenged me to have faith that God was working even though I couldn't see it. She encouraged me, in humility, to love those who were critical of me. She prayed for me and over me. She kept spurring me on in love. The results of her prayers and encouragement are visible in my life and ministry today. She was a Ruth to me, and God used her in tremendous ways. God gives grace to the humble. When we act in humility instead of demanding our own way, we are following the example of Christ who was gentle and humble in heart. I cannot begin to express the depths of love I feel for this amazing friend and her gentle accountability. Everybody needs a friend like Ruth. Who is yours?

Assignment Three

Obedient

After Ruth told Naomi all that happened to her at the field, Naomi instructed Ruth about what she should do next. Out of Ruth's humility we see her willingness to be obedient both to Naomi's somewhat bizarre request, and later to Boaz as well.

A woman of excellence is not only courageous and humble, she is also obedient. Write your understanding of what it means to be obedient here.

Although in Christ we have a relationship with God through faith, obedience is evidence of our faith in him. Ruth had a faith in God that made her teachable. She did not insist that she knew the best way to handle things. She presented her thoughts and desires with humility and responded as directed with obedience.

To be obedient means you are submissive to the restraint or command of authority. In essence we all obey something. In Romans 6:16, Paul says:

Do you not know that when you present yourselves to someone as slaves for obedience, you are slaves of the one whom you obey, either of sin resulting in death, or of obedience resulting in righteousness?

We are either slaves to the flesh and sin, or slaves to God. One leads to death, the other to righteousness. We get to choose. We can never underestimate the importance of obedience to the Scriptures and to the leading of the Holy Spirit in our journey of faith.

Read all of Ruth chapter three before you begin your study today.

1.   Briefly review the verses below. What was Ruth's response to Naomi's instructions? What does her response reveal about her character?

   1   *Then Naomi her mother-in-law said to her, "My daughter, shall I not seek security for you, that it may be well with you?*

   2   *Now is not Boaz our kinsman, with whose maids you were? Behold, he winnows barley at the threshing floor tonight.*

   3   *Wash yourself therefore, and anoint yourself and put on your best clothes, and go down to the threshing floor; but do not make yourself known to the man until he has finished eating and drinking.*

   4   *It shall be when he lies down, that you shall notice the place where he lies, and you shall go and uncover his feet and lie down; then he will tell you what you shall do."*

   5   *She said to her, "All that you say I will do."*

   6   *So she went down to the threshing floor and did according to all that her mother-in-law had commanded her. Ruth 3:1–6*

2. What does 1 John 5:3 tell us about obedience? Write out in your own words why obeying God's commands is not burdensome.

> 3   *This is love for God: to obey his commands. And his commands are not burdensome.* (NIV)

3. Obedience to God's will over our own is something we must choose daily. What does God say to us in Deuteronomy 30:15–18 about the importance of choosing to obey him? List the benefits of obedience and note the ones that mean the most to you.

> 15   *See, I set before you today life and prosperity, death and destruction.*
>
> 16   *For I command you today to love the LORD your God, to walk in his ways, and to keep his commands, decrees and laws; then you will live and increase, and the LORD your God will bless you in the land you are entering to possess.*
>
> 17   *But if your heart turns away and you are not obedient, and if you are drawn away to bow down to other gods and worship them,*
>
> 18   *I declare to you this day that you will certainly be destroyed. You will not live long in the land you are crossing the Jordan to enter and possess.* (NIV)

List the benefits here:

4. After Ruth went to Boaz at the threshing floor as Naomi instructed her, Boaz told Ruth what he intended to do for her. According to Ruth 3:11, what did Boaz tell Ruth about his people's opinion of her?

    11 *Now, my daughter, do not fear. I will do for you whatever you ask, for all my people in the city know that you are a woman of excellence.*

5. Actions often speak louder than words. Ruth's obedience led to her reputation among the Israelites in Bethlehem. Record your thoughts about what the Scripture means when it says that Ruth is a *woman of excellence?*

Something to Think About:

Obedience is a critical part of our faith walk. Scripture tells us that Jesus himself was obedient to the point of death. Obedience and discipleship go hand in hand.

Jesus called to some fishermen saying, *Come follow me.* To follow they had to be humbly willing to be led. Jesus calls us into the same relationship with him. We are to follow his lead, treat people as he treated people, and love God as he loved God. Living out these two greatest commandments is impossible if you are rebellious and un-teachable. One of the greatest lessons my parents ever taught me was to be obedient. It is the lesson I am trying to instill in my own children. I know that if they won't obey me, they will not learn the importance of obeying God. My question to you is simple: "Are you obedient and teachable?" Ask God to show you.

Wrapping it Up:

Becoming a woman of excellence is not a one-time overnight event. Instead it is a lifelong course. With each test, trial, triumph, or tragedy, we must learn to ask this all important question: "God, what do you want me to learn from this situation?" Most lessons in life have a two-fold purpose: to grow you in Christ-like character and to teach you more about God's faithfulness to you. If the lessons were easy we would never grow in our faith or our dependence upon him. The goal of each new experience is that you become more Christ-like in your actions and reactions. I can say without a doubt that Christ is faithful, loyal, determined, courageous, humble and obedient. How precious it is to know that becoming a woman of excellence is becoming like Jesus.

Practical Exercise

Choosing Faith Over Feelings. Faith is believing what is not yet seen (Heb. 11:1). Faith is necessary to please God (Heb. 11:6), and acting upon it (James 1:22–25) no matter how I feel (Heb. 11:17—I'm sure it hurt Abraham to think of sacrificing Isaac), because God rewards those who earnestly seek him (Heb. 11:6).

Ruth made many positive choices. She chose to stay with Naomi. She chose to listen to Naomi about gleaning in the fields and about Boaz. She chose to listen to Boaz. She chose to honor and worship God over the idols of Moab. She made choices that led to life while Naomi made choices that led to death.

Feelings play a big part in our decision-making process. Choosing the faithful thing over the feel good thing is an important lesson to learn.

Feelings can cause people to *do what is right in their own eyes* (Judges 17:6).

1.   Why do you think the following words are repeated in two different verses in Proverbs?

There is a way which seems right to a man and appears straight before him, but at the end of it is the way of death. (Proverbs 14:12, Proverbs 16:25 AMP)

2. Take some time this week to examine your thoughts and feelings (emotions) to see if your heart is seeking its own way or God's way.

    Is there an area of your life that you are failing to trust to God's way? Write out your thoughts or talk to God about what it would take to align your thoughts and actions with God's way instead of your own.

3. Read Hebrews 11:6 paying careful attention to the last phrase: *And without faith it is impossible to please God, because anyone who comes to him must believe that he exists and that he rewards <u>those who earnestly seek him</u>* (NIV).

    Write out your thoughts to the Lord, or share with an accountability sister how you will proceed in this area to honor God and follow him.

Study Group Questions

1. What are the ways that Ruth showed her courage?

2. Discuss what true humility is and what it is not.

3. Why do you think the character trait of humility is so rare today?

4. Why do you think we sometimes get it wrong when we "try to be humble"? How can trying to be humble look like pride instead?

5. How would our lives look if we lived every day according to Philippians 2:3-4? How might this focus transform our lives from prideful to humble?

6. How do you think obeying God's commands can be considered not burdensome?

7. Discuss some practical everyday things that can help make obeying God our habit of daily life.

NOTES

LESSON SEVEN:

Boaz, the Kinsman-redeemer—Part One

Hope. It is the one thing that is absolutely necessary to keep us going in the midst of our tests, trials and tragedies. Early on in Ruth, Naomi insisted that her daughters-in-law return to their families in Moab. She said to the girls in Ruth 1:11–13:

11 *But Naomi said, "Return, my daughters. Why should you go with me? Have I yet sons in my womb, that they may be your husbands?*

12 *Return, my daughters! Go, for I am too old to have a husband. If I said I have hope, if I should even have a husband tonight and also bear sons,*

13 *would you therefore wait until they were grown? Would you therefore refrain from marrying? No, my daughters; for it is harder for me than for you, for the hand of the LORD has gone forth against me."*

During the times in which Naomi lived, widows without living heirs (sons) had to depend upon a kinsman-redeemer, a brother or near relative to the deceased husband to provide an heir and protect his name from being blotted out from Israel (Deut. 25:5–10). Naomi believed she was too old to remarry and have more children. She saw her circumstances as hopeless—the obstacles to finding a kinsman-redeemer were overwhelming. But then a man of incredible character, Boaz, a kinsman, or near (close) relative of Naomi's husband, entered into the lives of these poor, hurting women. His actions instilled in both Naomi and Ruth the belief that their lives could somehow be different. Perhaps all was not lost. Suddenly a hopeless Naomi began to hope in a better future and the possibility of a redeemed life in Israel.

In this lesson we'll explore how the Godly character of their kinsman encouraged Ruth and Naomi to rise above their devastating circumstances and look forward to a better life. Before we get started let's define kinsman and explore his role in the clan.

As you read the definition for "kinsman" in the Word Study box on the next page, underline any words or phrases that help you better understand the role and responsibilities of a "kinsman-redeemer."

WORD STUDY

Kinsman

The Hebrew word for "kinsman" is *ga'al* pronounced gaw•al. A kinsman was the nearest living male blood relation. The Strong's definition defines the role of the kinsman: to redeem, act as kinsman-redeemer, avenge, revenge, ransom, do the part of a kinsman.

The kinsman has several responsibilities such as:

- To act as kinsman, do the part of next of kin, act as kinsman-redeemer by marrying a brother's widow to beget a child for him.

- To redeem from slavery.

- To redeem land.

- To exact vengeance.*

As you can see from the definition, the kinsman played an important role in family life. A kinsman who obeyed the law and embraced his responsibility could literally change the course of a destitute family member's life.

* Strong, J. (1996). *The exhaustive concordance of the Bible.*

Assignment One

Boaz the Protector

God's goodness is plainly seen in the law when in Deuteronomy 25:5-10 he made specific provision for widows through the kinsman. In our assignment today we'll continue to look in the Book of Ruth to see the first role of the kinsman—protector.

When the two women arrived in Bethlehem, Naomi believed she was too old to marry again. Ruth, being of Moabite heritage, did not have good prospects for remarriage either. As widows in Bethlehem, Naomi and Ruth had no one to support them. Ruth committed to gleaning the fields to provide food. The fields could be a dangerous place. Ruth would need someone to protect her.

1. Read Ruth 2:1-9a and 15 on the next page. As you read, underline the words and phrases that help you see Boaz's protection. Make note of what you learn about Boaz in the space provided. How does the Scripture describe him? What does he say to his reapers? What does that reveal about his character?

1   Now Naomi had a kinsman of her husband, a man of great wealth, of the family of Elimelech, whose name was Boaz.

2   And Ruth the Moabitess said to Naomi, "Please let me go to the field and glean among the ears of grain after one in whose sight I may find favor." And she said to her, "Go, my daughter."

3   So she departed and went and gleaned in the field after the reapers; and she happened to come to the portion of the field belonging to Boaz, who was of the family of Elimelech.

4   Now behold, Boaz came from Bethlehem and said to the reapers, "May the LORD be with you." And they said to him, "May the LORD bless you."

5   Then Boaz said to his servant who was in charge of the reapers, "Whose young woman is this?"

6   The servant in charge of the reapers replied, "She is the young Moabite woman who returned with Naomi from the land of Moab.

7   "And she said, 'Please let me glean and gather after the reapers among the sheaves.' Thus she came and has remained from the morning until now; she has been sitting in the house for a little while."

8   Then Boaz said to Ruth, "Listen carefully, my daughter. Do not go to glean in another field; furthermore, do not go on from this one, but stay here with my maids.

9   "Let your eyes be on the field which they reap, and go after them. Indeed, I have commanded the servants not to touch you.

15   When she rose to glean, Boaz commanded his servants, saying, "Let her glean even among the sheaves, and do not insult her.

What I learn about Boaz:

2. Perhaps recognizing his family responsibility caused Boaz to immediately take action to protect Ruth. List the two types of protection given to Ruth in verses 9, and 15.

    • Boaz provided _____ protection for young Ruth commanding that the servant not lay a hand on her.

- In verse 15, Boaz provided protection from _____ insults.

Remember, not only was Ruth a young woman, she was also a Moabitess. The physical protection made it safe for her to work in the fields. Just as important was the protection from the verbal insults. Often words can cause us to feel just as unsafe as physical threats. Words can cut and wound. It is beautiful that Boaz recognized how both threats might affect Ruth.

3. His protection required that Ruth follow three specific instructions in Ruth 2:8-9. What were they?

- _____

- _____

- _____

4. What connection do you see between protection and obedience?

5. In Ruth 2:12 Boaz said to Ruth:

12 *May the LORD reward your work, and your wages be full from the LORD, the God of Israel, under whose wings you have come to seek refuge.*

Boaz recognized that Ruth had come to Israel seeking God's shelter. In Hebrew the word shelter is often used of those seeking protection and security from God. Boaz recognized Ruth was trusting in God and God used him to ensure her safety. Just as Ruth expected God would protect her, we too can expect God will protect us. Read Psalm 91:1-2 and answer the questions that follow.

1 *He who dwells in the shelter of the Most High Will abide in the shadow of the Almighty.*

2 *I will say to the LORD, "My refuge and my fortress, My God, in whom I trust!"*

- Where do you seek refuge when you need to feel safe?

- What confidence does Psalm 91:1-2 give you as you face life's trials and tests?

- How can knowing that God protects you help you overcome tests and trials?

Something to Think About:

In my life, feeling protected makes me feel secure. Ruth was in a foreign land with people who had a poor opinion of Moabites. She ventured out to provide food for herself and her mother-in-law, Naomi, at great personal risk. What I love about Ruth is that she did not have to feel protected before she took a step of faith. Instead she stepped out in faith, trusting God to provide protection. God used the obedient and faithful man, Boaz, as her protector. In the midst of life's tests, trials, and tragedies, do you step out in faith believing God will protect you?

One of the biggest lessons from Ruth's life is that God will meet you more than half way when you step out in faith. Perhaps you need to have a difficult conversation with someone. Step out in faith and believe that God will protect you and shelter you. Do you feel called to change jobs but fear is keeping you from taking a risk? Step out in faith and trust that God will protect you under the shadow of his wings. Are you afraid because you've recently experienced a divorce? Take a step of faith to start living again, trust God to protect your heart.

Assignment Two

Boaz the Provider

Naomi and Ruth were two poor destitute widows. God made provisions for the needy, saying in Leviticus 19:9-10:

9   *Now when you reap the harvest of your land, you shall not reap to the very corners of your field, nor shall you gather the gleanings of your harvest.*

10   *Nor shall you glean your vineyard, nor shall you gather the fallen fruit of your vineyard; you shall leave them for the needy and for the stranger. I am the LORD your God.*

Naomi and Ruth would survive. The work of gleaning would be too difficult for Naomi, but Ruth was able to work the long hours for food. Through it all, Ruth knew the Lord cared. He cared enough about her hunger that he commanded provision be made. Not only does God demonstrate his care in Scripture, he also moves the hearts of those who follow him to care for others as well. In Boaz we see a man who went over and above what was required of him.

1. Read Ruth 2:9b, 14–18, and 3:15–17. Circle ways Boaz provided for Ruth and Naomi's physical needs. List what you find in the space provided.

Ruth 2

9b When you are thirsty, go to the water jars and drink from what the servants draw."

14 At mealtime Boaz said to her, "Come here, that you may eat of the bread and dip your piece of bread in the vinegar." So she sat beside the reapers; and he served her roasted grain, and she ate and was satisfied and had some left.

15 When she rose to glean, Boaz commanded his servants, saying, "Let her glean even among the sheaves, and do not insult her.

16 "Also you shall purposely pull out for her some grain from the bundles and leave it that she may glean, and do not rebuke her."

17 So she gleaned in the field until evening. Then she beat out what she had gleaned, and it was about an ephah of barley.

18 She took it up and went into the city, and her mother-in-law saw what she had gleaned. She also took it out and gave Naomi what she had left after she was satisfied.

Ruth 3

15 Again he said, "Give me the cloak that is on you and hold it." So she held it, and he measured six measures of barley and laid it on her. Then she went into the city.

16 When she came to her mother-in-law, she said, "How did it go, my daughter?" And she told her all that the man had done for her.

17 She said, "These six measures of barley he gave to me, for he said, 'Do not go to your mother-in-law empty-handed.' "

Verse	Physical Needs

In the same way Boaz saw Naomi and Ruth's needs, the Lord sees and provides for all our needs. He is our supply, our water when we thirst, our bread when we are hungry, and he cares about all our needs. He is always working on our behalf to provide and care for us even though we may not see it or know it. For example, look at what was happening behind the scenes. After asking Naomi if she could go and glean in the fields, we read this all important passage: *and she happened to come to the portion of the field belonging to Boaz, who was of the family of Elimelech* (Ruth 2:3).

What an amazing development. Ruth had no idea whose field she was being led to. God guided her to Boaz's field. We know from chapter 3, Ruth did not know Boaz, his relation to Naomi, or where his fields were. It was Naomi who told Ruth who Boaz was. God used Boaz to provide for Naomi and Ruth.

2. Read Matthew 6:25–34:

25 *That is why I tell you not to worry about everyday life—whether you have enough food and drink, or enough clothes to wear. Isn't life more than food, and your body more than clothing?*

26 *Look at the birds. They don't plant or harvest or store food in barns, for your heavenly Father feeds them. And aren't you far more valuable to him than they are?*

27 *Can all your worries add a single moment to your life?*

28 *"And why worry about your clothing? Look at the lilies of the field and how they grow. They don't work or make their clothing,*

29 *yet Solomon in all his glory was not dressed as beautifully as they are.*

30 And if God cares so wonderfully for wildflowers that are here today and thrown into the fire tomorrow, he will certainly care for you. Why do you have so little faith?

31 So don't worry about these things, saying, "What will we eat? What will we drink? What will we wear?"

32 These things dominate the thoughts of unbelievers, but your heavenly Father already knows all your needs.

33 Seek the Kingdom of God above all else, and live righteously, and he will give you everything you need.

34 So don't worry about tomorrow, for tomorrow will bring its own worries. Today's trouble is enough for today. (NLT)

How do these words offer you confidence for times when you face trials and tests in your life? Write your thoughts here:

3. Based on Ruth 2:3 and Matthew 6:25-34 above, what part does God play in meeting your needs?

4. Why do you think Jesus connects worry with having little faith in his care for you in Matthew 6:25-34?

What does Jesus say about worry?

5. How can seeing God as your provider encourage you to overcome worry in the midst of tests and trials?

Something to Think About:

Provision. I know right now in the difficult times in which we live, some of you are wondering where your provision is going to come from. Please believe that God is at work. He sees every detail of your life and is working to provide for and protect you. I know it is difficult to wait on his plan to unfold. While you wait, ask him to show you what he wants you to learn from your current test or trial. Remember, what God wants most is for you to have an intimate relationship with him. Through the testing, he wants you to learn that he is dependable and faithful.

Assignment Three

Glimmers of Change

In the midst of sorrow and hardship God's handprint was slowly becoming visible. Hope was beginning to rise. Glimpses of God and his goodness could be seen where once Naomi could only see emptiness and sorrow. Today we're going to look at how Boaz's protection and provision broke down the walls of embittered Naomi—a woman who wanted only to be called Mara—and at the same time comforted young Ruth.

Comfort:

1. Read Ruth 2:10–13 on the next page.

10 Then she fell on her face, bowing to the ground and said to him, "Why have I found favor in your sight that you should take notice of me, since I am a foreigner?"

11 Boaz replied to her, "All that you have done for your mother-in-law after the death of your husband has been fully reported to me, and how you left your father and your mother and the land of your birth, and came to a people that you did not previously know.

12 May the LORD reward your work, and your wages be full from the LORD, the God of Israel, under whose wings you have come to seek refuge."

13 Then she said, "I have found favor in your sight, my lord, for you have comforted me and indeed have spoken kindly to your maidservant, though I am not like one of your maidservants."

Ruth found favor with Boaz because of the way she cared for Naomi. What affect did Boaz's words have on Ruth?

2. To comfort is to console someone, causing them to feel less unhappy. According to verse 11 when did Ruth begin to demonstrate her care for Naomi?

3. Ruth had experienced the same tragedies as Naomi. She too was heartbroken. Why do you think Boaz's words comforted Ruth?

4. Read Psalm 34:17–19 and Psalm 147:3:

 17   *The LORD hears his people when they call to him for help. He rescues them from all their troubles.*

 18   *The LORD is close to the brokenhearted; he rescues those whose spirits are crushed.*

 19   *The righteous person faces many troubles, but the LORD comes to the rescue each time.* (NLT)

  3   *He heals the brokenhearted and bandages their wounds.*

• What does the Lord promise his people?

• What verse encourages you the most and why?

Something to Think About:

I imagine Boaz's words of comfort penetrated right through to Ruth's soul. She may have still been mourning the loss of her husband and the dream of living happily ever after. She left her family behind. She lost her home and all she and her husband had worked for while they were married. But because of her love for Naomi, Ruth refused to leave her mother-in-law. Instead she immediately began the task of caring for their needs, putting herself at risk, doing back-breaking work in the fields, and carrying the food back to town.

On the long walks to and from work perhaps her mind wandered to all she had lost. Did anyone notice that she was hurting as Naomi was? Did anyone care? It is no wonder that Boaz's kindhearted words brought her comfort. Someone noticed she had lost her husband; someone noticed she was doing her best to care for Naomi. Someone did care; someone saw her pain. It was Boaz. Boaz recognized her situation and offered her words of encouragement and comfort. He saw her rising above her circumstances and overcoming her pain. His words were life giving. His words not only encouraged Ruth, but they also had an affect on Naomi.

Hope:

1. Read Ruth 2:18–22:

    18 *She took it up and went into the city, and her mother-in-law saw what she had gleaned. She also took it out and gave Naomi what she had left after she was satisfied.*

    19 *Her mother-in-law then said to her, "Where did you glean today and where did you work? May he who took notice of you be blessed." So she told her mother-in-law with whom she had worked and said, "The name of the man with whom I worked today is Boaz."*

    20 *Naomi said to her daughter-in-law, "May he be blessed of the LORD who has not withdrawn his kindness to the living and to the dead." Again Naomi said to her, "The man is our relative, he is one of our closest relatives."*

    21 *Then Ruth the Moabitess said, "Furthermore, he said to me, 'You should stay close to my servants until they have finished all my harvest.' "*

    22 *Naomi said to Ruth her daughter-in-law, "It is good, my daughter, that you go out with his maids, so that others do not fall upon you in another field."*

    Hope is the most important ingredient to overcoming life's tests and trials. Without it, one is tempted to give up in life. Hopelessness happens when we set our minds on the temporary. Naomi had been focused on how hopeless her situation appeared. It has been said that you need hope to cope.

    You can almost hear the change in Naomi's voice as she realized that Ruth had been led to the field of Boaz, her kinsman. What does she say about Boaz in chapter 2, verse 20, and why do you think her words are significant?

2. What affect do you think Boaz's kindness had on Naomi's outlook for the future?

3. Read Ruth 3:16–18. Boaz did not want Ruth to return to Naomi empty handed. Compare this passage with Ruth 1:21. What affect do you think this gesture had on Naomi's faith in God?

> 16 When she came to her mother-in-law, she said, "How did it go, my daughter?" And she told her all that the man had done for her.
>
> 17 She said, "These six measures of barley he gave to me, for he said, 'Do not go to your mother-in-law empty-handed.' "
>
> 18 Then she said, "Wait, my daughter, until you know how the matter turns out; for the man will not rest until he has settled it today."

4. According to Psalm 62:5–8, what should be the source of our hope?

> 5 My soul, wait in silence for God only, For my hope is from Him.
>
> 6 He only is my rock and my salvation, My stronghold; I shall not be shaken.
>
> 7 On God my salvation and my glory rest; The rock of my strength, my refuge is in God.
>
> 8 Trust in Him at all times, O people; Pour out your heart before Him; God is a refuge for us. Selah.

- What are the benefits of hoping in God according to this passage?

- What two things does verse 8 encourage us to do?

- When are we to trust in God? Are you able to trust in him at all times? Why or why not?

Something to Think About:

When we are lacking in hope it is often because we have taken our eyes off the Lord and focused our vision solely on the test, trial, or tragedy before us. To maintain the hope we need for each day we must learn to see God in our circumstances. God is bigger than our heartache and he is bigger than our trouble. When we feel ourselves slipping into hopelessness we can pour our hearts out to him. As we pray, our heart will remember to trust in him despite what we see. Remember, hopelessness happens when we set our hearts on the temporary. Hope happens when we set our hearts on the eternal.

Wrapping it Up:

Boaz did the right thing for the right reasons; he didn't choose to ignore the needs of others, but quickly moved to meet their needs in the right way. Boaz's protection and provision for Ruth and Naomi had a profound effect in each of their lives. Comfort and hope are important if we are going to overcome our tests and trials. I love that God will bring people into our lives to minister to us and provide for our needs. Boaz was God's hands and feet in Naomi and Ruth's lives. Next week we will continue to look at how God used Boaz to change the course of their lives.

Study Group Questions

1. Discuss the role of a kinsman-redeemer in Ruth and Naomi's day.

2. How do you see God at work in the lives of Naomi, Ruth, and Boaz in this lesson?

3. Based on Isaiah 61:1-3 and what you know about Jesus Christ's role for mankind, do you see any similarities in Jesus' role and that of the kinsman-redeemer? Think about the roles of a protector and a provider. How did each of them fulfill these roles?

4. Discuss some thoughts about God's willingness to be our comforter and provider. How does this make you feel?

5. What are some reasons we sometimes fail to recognize that all we have is provided by God alone? How can being intentionally grateful change our perspective and attitude?

6. How can having our needs met fill us with encouragement and hope? Why is this important for our sense of peace?

7. Remember, hopelessness happens when we set our hearts on the temporary. Hope happens when we set our hearts on the eternal. Discuss some ways we can practice keeping our focus on eternal things instead of rehearsing the pain of our temporary circumstances. (See Rom. 12:1-2 and 2 Cor. 1:4-5 for help.)

NOTES

LESSON EIGHT:

Boaz, the Kinsman-redeemer—Part Two

In the last lesson we looked at how Boaz's protection and provision for Naomi and Ruth affected their lives. Hopelessness and despair were replaced by comfort and hope. Naomi and Ruth began to hope in a different future. This week we will continue to look at the role Boaz played in their lives.

A very important role in the family life of Israel was that of the kinsman-redeemer. A kinsman who obeyed the law and embraced his responsibility could literally change the course of someone's life. As an instrument of change, a kinsman redeemed his brother's widow and, in doing so, restore their lives—their position, the family legacy, their hope, and their joy.

Assignment One

Boaz, the Kinsman-redeemer

Deuteronomy 25:5–6 says:

5   *When brothers live together and one of them dies and has no son, the wife of the deceased shall not be married outside the family to a strange man. Her husband's brother shall go in to her and take her to himself as wife and perform the duty of a husband's brother to her.*

6   *It shall be that the firstborn whom she bears shall assume the name of his dead brother, so that his name will not be blotted out from Israel.*

Using a dictionary or dictionary.com define the word redeem.

As we learned in *Lesson Seven*, the Hebrew word for redeemer is *ga'al*, meaning to redeem, avenge, ransom, and do the part of a kinsman. *The Theological Wordbook of the Old Testament, Volume 1* adds to the definition saying:

"The primary meaning of this root is to do the part of a kinsman and thus to redeem his kin from difficulty or danger. It is used with its derivatives 118 times [...] there is usually an emphasis in *ga'al* on the redemption being the privilege or duty of a near relative."

Without a redeemer, Naomi's husband's name would be blotted out from Israel; she and Ruth would be poor destitute widows with no hope of a happy future. In Ruth 4:14 the women of Bethlehem give us insight into the importance of a redeemer for Naomi.

14   *Then the women said to Naomi, "Blessed is the LORD who has not left you without a redeemer today and may his name become famous in Israel."*

Let's explore how Boaz came to redeem Naomi and Ruth.

1.   Read Ruth 3:6–14:

6   *So she went down to the threshing floor and did according to all that her mother-in-law had commanded her.*

7   *When Boaz had eaten and drunk and his heart was merry, he went to lie down at the end of the heap of grain; and she came secretly, and uncovered his feet and lay down.*

8   *It happened in the middle of the night that the man was startled and bent forward; and behold, a woman was lying at his feet.*

9   *He said, "Who are you?" And she answered, "I am Ruth your maid. So spread your covering over your maid, for you are a close relative."*

10   *Then he said, "May you be blessed of the LORD, my daughter. You have shown your last kindness to be better than the first by not going after young men, whether poor or rich.*

11   *Now, my daughter, do not fear. I will do for you whatever you ask, for all my people in the city know that you are a woman of excellence.*

12   *Now it is true I am a close relative; however, there is a relative closer than I.*

13   *Remain this night, and when morning comes, if he will redeem you, good; let him redeem you. But if he does not wish to redeem you, then I will redeem you, as the LORD lives. Lie down until morning."*

14   *So she lay at his feet until morning and rose before one could recognize another; and he said, "Let it not be known that the woman came to the threshing floor."*

What do you think Ruth was asking of Boaz in this passage?

2. Look up Ezekiel 16:8 in your Bible. What further insight does this passage give you into what Ruth was asking of Boaz?

3. What does Boaz promise Ruth in verse 11–13?

4. To overcome her circumstances, Ruth had to step out obediently and follow Naomi's instructions. What do you think she learned from her step of faith?

5. What do you think verse 10 reveals about how Ruth's request affected Boaz?

Something to Think About:

Ruth and Naomi placed their hope in a kinsman-redeemer who had the power to act on their behalf and change their circumstances. In order to overcome our circumstances and get beyond our tests, trials and tragedies, we often have to step out in faith. Steps of faith often feel risky. But if we want to overcome our circumstances we have to put aside our fears. Ruth and Naomi's only hope for a better life was trusting that their kinsman-redeemer would be faithful to his promise.

Assignment Two

Promise Keeper

How many times has someone promised to do something on your behalf and not followed through? Being able to trust in someone's word is so important.

1. Read Ruth 4:1–10, 13:

>   1   Now Boaz went up to the gate and sat down there, and behold, the close relative of whom Boaz spoke was passing by, so he said, "Turn aside, friend, sit down here." And he turned aside and sat down.
>
>   2   He took ten men of the elders of the city and said, "Sit down here." So they sat down.
>
>   3   Then he said to the closest relative, "Naomi, who has come back from the land of Moab, has to sell the piece of land which belonged to our brother Elimelech.
>
>   4   So I thought to inform you, saying, 'Buy it before those who are sitting here, and before the elders of my people. If you will redeem it, redeem it; but if not, tell me that I may know; for there is no one but you to redeem it, and I am after you.' " And he said, "I will redeem it."
>
>   5   Then Boaz said, "On the day you buy the field from the hand of Naomi, you must also acquire Ruth the Moabitess, the widow of the deceased, in order to raise up the name of the deceased on his inheritance."
>
>   6   The closest relative said, "I cannot redeem it for myself, because I would jeopardize my own inheritance. Redeem it for yourself; you may have my right of redemption, for I cannot redeem it."

7   *Now this was the custom in former times in Israel concerning the redemption and the exchange of land to confirm any matter: a man removed his sandal and gave it to another; and this was the manner of attestation in Israel.*

8   *So the closest relative said to Boaz, "Buy it for yourself." And he removed his sandal.*

9   *Then Boaz said to the elders and all the people, "You are witnesses today that I have bought from the hand of Naomi all that belonged to Elimelech and all that belonged to Chilion and Mahlon.*

10 *Moreover, I have acquired Ruth the Moabitess, the widow of Mahlon, to be my wife in order to raise up the name of the deceased on his inheritance, so that the name of the deceased will not be cut off from his brothers or from the court of his birth place; you are witnesses today."*

13 *So Boaz took Ruth, and she became his wife, and he went in to her. And the LORD enabled her to conceive, and she gave birth to a son.*

What action did Boaz take on behalf of Naomi?

2.   How did the redemption of Elimelech's land affect Ruth?

3.   According to verse 10, what would have happened had the land not been redeemed?

4. What was the end result of Boaz redeeming the land (see verse 13 for help)?

5. What similarities do you see in Naomi and Ruth's need for a redeemer and ours?

Something to Think About:

While we have looked at the definition of redeem, I think it is important at this point to revisit it. To redeem something or someone not only means to buy back, it also means to free from what distresses or harms, to help to overcome something detrimental, and to change for the better. In the case of Naomi and Ruth their redeemer helped them to overcome what had distressed them; he helped them overcome the detrimental condition of poverty and changed their lives for the better.

Assignment Three

Restorer

Naomi encouraged Ruth to ask Boaz to redeem her and he kept the promise he made to her at the threshing floor. He was able to restore to them their position in the family line by providing an heir. But there was so much more their redeemer did that transformed their lives. When we are going through tests, trials and tragedies it is comforting to know that there is someone who is faithful to his promises, dependable, and has the power to transform even seemingly hopeless situations.

Today we will look at how Boaz restored and transformed the lives of Ruth and Naomi.

1. Read Ruth 4:13–17a:

    13 So Boaz took Ruth, and she became his wife, and he went in to her. And the Lord enabled her to conceive, and she gave birth to a son.

    14 Then the women said to Naomi, "Blessed is the Lord who has not left you without a redeemer today, and may his name become famous in Israel.

    15 May he also be to you a restorer of life and a sustainer of your old age; for your daughter-in-law, who loves you and is better to you than seven sons, has given birth to him."

    16 Then Naomi took the child and laid him in her lap, and became his nurse.

    17 The neighbor women gave him a name, saying, "A son has been born to Naomi!" So they named him Obed...

When Boaz and Ruth had a child, that child carried her former husband's name—Mahlon's name. The baby therefore became Naomi's grandchild by law (see verse 17). What a reversal of circumstances; Naomi went from childless to Grandma Naomi.

- Look again at verses 13–15. Who are the women talking about?

- What blessing did the women ask of God regarding the baby?

2. Compare verse 16 with Ruth 1:20–21 below.

    20 She said to them, "Do not call me Naomi; call me Mara, for the Almighty has dealt very bitterly with me.

    21 I went out full, but the LORD has brought me back empty. Why do you call me Naomi, since the LORD has witnessed against me and the Almighty has afflicted me?"

- What differences do you see in Naomi from chapter one to chapter four in regard to her emotions?

- What differences do you see in Naomi from chapter one to chapter four in regard to her situation?

When we see the work of the kinsman-redeemer in Naomi and Ruth's lives we can't help but long for a kinsman-redeemer to act on our behalf. Someone whose love and kindness could help us rise above our circumstances and give us hope for a better life. Perhaps that is why God included the Book of Ruth in the Bible, so we might recognize the importance of a redeemer in our own lives. Boaz is identified by scholars as a *type* of Christ.

Review below the definitions of type and prefigure.

ENGLISH WORD DEFINITION
Type and Prefigure

Type–noun

1. the pattern or model from which something is made.
2. an image or figure produced by impressing or stamping, as the principal figure or device on either side of a coin or medal.
3. a distinctive or characteristic mark or sign.
4. a symbol of something in the future, as an Old Testament event serving as a prefiguration of a new testament event.

Prefigure–verb (used with object), -ured, -ur•ing

1. to show or represent beforehand by a figure or type; foreshadow.
2. to picture or represent to oneself beforehand; imagine.

Definitions taken from: Dictionary.com at http://dictionary.reference.com/browse/type

---

3.   Before we go on, reflect over what you have learned about a kinsman-redeemer up to this point. In what ways do you think that Boaz prefigured Christ?

4. Compare what you know about Boaz with what you learn in the following passage about Christ, our Redeemer. What similarities do you see between Boaz and Jesus Christ?

1   *Bless the LORD, O my soul,*

    And all that is within me, bless His holy name.

2   *Bless the LORD, O my soul,*

    And forget none of His benefits;

3   *Who pardons all your iniquities,*

    Who heals all your diseases;

4   *Who redeems your life from the pit,*

    Who crowns you with lovingkindness and compassion;

5   *Who satisfies your years with good things,*

    So that your youth is renewed like the eagle. Psalm 103:1-5

Record your comparisons of Boaz and Jesus here:

Naomi's Transformation

Through the birth of Obed, Boaz restored the family name of Naomi's husband and sons, her position, and her joy. In fact, verse 16 is a picture of pure joy. Naomi had experienced great loss and horrible emotional pain in her life. But now, through the marriage of Ruth and the birth of Obed, her hope, joy, comfort, security, and position had all been restored. Her life was completely transformed by her redeemer.

Now let's look at the effect Boaz's actions had on Ruth. We've seen that he took her to be his wife and they had a son. But note something that is equally important—Ruth's new identity.

5. Read the following passages. Pay special attention to the name attached to Ruth.

    22 *So Naomi returned, and with her Ruth the Moabitess, her daughter-in-law, who returned from the land of Moab. And they came to Bethlehem at the beginning of barley harvest.* Ruth 1:22

    4   *Now behold, Boaz came from Bethlehem and said to the reapers, "May the LORD be with you." And they said to him, "May the LORD bless you."*

    5   *Then Boaz said to his servant who was in charge of the reapers, "Whose young woman is this?"*

    6   *The servant in charge of the reapers replied, "She is the young Moabite woman who returned with Naomi from the land of Moab."* Ruth 2:4–6

    How is Ruth identified by the narrator and the servant in charge of the reapers?

6. Ruth is referred to as the Moabitess five times throughout the book. Based on what you have learned about Moab, what point do you think the author is trying to make regarding her identity?

7. Read Ruth 3:11:

    11 *Now, my daughter, do not fear. I will do for you whatever you ask, for all my people in the city know that you are a woman of excellence.*

What does Boaz call Ruth in this verse?

8. When the term is used of a woman, the Hebrew word for excellence is translated "virtuous" in the ASV Bible and "worthy" or "good" in RSV. It is only used two other times in Scripture to describe a woman. Read the passages below and note the Hebrew word for excellence which is underlined.

    A wife of <u>noble</u> character is her husband's crown, but a disgraceful wife is like decay in his bones. Proverbs 12:4 (NIV)

    Who can find a <u>virtuous</u> woman? For her price is far above rubies. Proverbs 31:10 (KJV)

    What further insight do these two verses give you concerning Ruth's character?

9. How important do you think it was for Ruth to have a new identity?

Something to Think About:

It was through great personal tragedy that Ruth recognized her heart for God. She refused to return to the idols of her people and instead confessed her faith in Naomi's God. God used her tragic heartbreak to bring her to a place where her life could be redeemed by her kinsman-redeemer.

From Ruth the Moabitess, to Ruth a woman of excellence, she is an example to others of selfless love and devotion! It was through the fire of her trials that her character was proven. What an amazing transformation this represented for Ruth. Love and devotion for Naomi proved Ruth's faith in the God of Israel. No one could dispute the evidence of her transformation. By calling her a woman of excellence and then taking her to be his wife, Boaz forever transformed the identity of Ruth.

Wrapping it Up:

Boaz, the kinsman-redeemer, transformed the lives of Ruth and Naomi, who were once devastated and hopeless as a result of the tests and trials of life; now each experienced a new beginning. The self-described empty Naomi, who had changed her name to Mara, or bitter, now experienced the joy of a new family. Young Ruth the Moabitess was no longer an outcast widowed foreigner; she was now considered a woman of excellence and the wife of Boaz. Their kinsman-redeemer had been faithful to his word and his duty. As a result these two women's lives would forever be different, even better. Their tests and trials had broken them, but God was with them guiding them to a better life through Boaz's obedience. As you can see, the kinsman-redeemer played an important role in the life of the children of Israel. Boaz is known as a *type* of Christ. His role in the lives of Naomi and Ruth is similar to the role of Christ in our lives. Just as Boaz was Ruth's kinsman-redeemer, so Christ is ours.

Study Group Questions

1. Discuss what you understand about the role of the kinsman-redeemer. Why do you think God put this practice in place?

2. Talk about the benefits each of the women gained from Boaz's decision to redeem Elimelech's land and to take Ruth as his wife.

3. What did it mean for Ruth to be called a woman of excellence in Bethlehem of Judah?

4. What makes someone a woman of excellence? What would it take for us to become known as women of excellence?

5. For us today, what is the significance of Jesus Christ being our redeemer?

NOTES

LESSON NINE:

New Beginnings

One of the most profound statements in the Book of Ruth goes almost unnoticed. It simply reads, *And they came to Bethlehem at the beginning of barley harvest* (Ruth 1:22). There is an important lesson to be explored in this simple sentence. We must never forget that the end of one thing is always the beginning of another. No matter what tests, trials and tragedies we encounter, there will always be a new beginning that follows. In fact, Jesus, our kinsman-redeemer, is all about new beginnings.

In this lesson we will explore how the Lord will use our tests, trials and tragedies to refine our character as he gives us more of himself. We will also see how he gives us beauty for ashes.

Assignment One

From Ashes to Beauty

Naomi and Ruth probably wondered why they faced the tragedies. They likely asked: "Why God, did you allow this to happen in our lives?" "How can we ever get past it?" "How could life ever be good again?"

It is not unusual for us to ask the same questions. While we may never know why God has allowed us to go through a difficult painful time, we can be assured that his will is for our good and not our harm. God doesn't want us to stay locked in our pain and heartbreak. Instead, he wants us to surrender our feelings and be set free to move beyond the past.

1. Isaiah 61:1–4 is a prophecy about Jesus, our redeemer, and his work in our lives.

   1 *The Spirit of the Sovereign LORD is upon me, for the LORD has anointed me to bring good news to the poor. He has sent me to comfort the brokenhearted and to proclaim that captives will be released and prisoners will be freed.*

   2 *He has sent me to tell those who mourn that the time of the LORD's favor has come, and with it, the day of God's anger against their enemies.*

   3 *To all who mourn in Israel, he will give a crown of beauty for ashes, a joyous blessing instead of mourning, festive praise instead of despair. In their righteousness, they will be like great oaks that the LORD has planted for his own glory.*

   4 *Then they will rebuild the ancient ruins, They will raise up the former devastations; And they will repair the ruined cities, The desolations of many generations.* (NLT)

   - What promises do these verses make regarding Jesus Christ's role in the lives of his people?

   - Reread verse three. What does the Lord promise to give all who mourn?

   - What does verse 3 imply will be the end result of our trials, tests and tragedies?

   - How do you think our experiences could be for his glory?

   Reread Isaiah 61:1–4 one more time. We give God our ashes, he gives us beauty. We give him our mourning, and he gives us blessing. Instead of despair, we can praise him from our hearts. Notice this: God always trades up!

2. See 2 Corinthians 4:16–18 below. What do these verses teach us about our troubles?

16 *Therefore we do not lose heart. Though outwardly we are wasting away, yet inwardly we are being renewed day by day.*

17 *For our light and momentary troubles are achieving for us an eternal glory that far outweighs them all.*

18 *So we fix our eyes not on what is seen, but on what is unseen. For what is seen is temporary, but what is unseen is eternal.* (NIV)

• How are our troubles described in this passage?

• What do troubles achieve for us according to verse 17?

• What should we fix our eyes on according to verse 18?

3. How does this passage encourage you as you go through tests, trials and troubles?

4. Look back at your *Experience Tree* on page 40. How do you see that God has given you beauty for ashes?

In what ways have you grown since the test, trial or tragedy?

5. Isaiah 61:3 says, *In their righteousness, they will be like great oaks that the Lord has planted for his own glory.* How can your righteous behavior in difficult times reveal God's glory?

6. Read 2 Corinthians 4:16–18, looking carefully at verse 18. What does focusing on the unseen look like in everyday life?

Something to Think About:

In the midst of our struggles it is so hard to see how God could possibly bring good from hardship. God knows that sometimes all we can do is put one foot in front of the other. He knows it is hard. But time and distance often bring new clarity. In some cases I can look back and clearly see God's hand and help during dark and trying times. But, my friends, there are a few things in my life that I am walking through now that I can't help but wonder why.

> *For You are my lamp, O Lord; And the Lord illumines my darkness.*
> 2 Samuel 22:29

Don't be tempted to think that the trial you are experiencing is caused by God. That would make God evil. God doesn't cause bad things to happen to you. He allows them to happen so that by walking through them you might reach out for his hand and grow <u>in your dependance on him</u>. He wants to walk through the difficulties with you. He wants to use tough times for our good—the strengthening of our faith and the maturing of our character.

We've talked at length about what God wants to do for you in your trials and how he wants to give you more of himself. My sweet friend, look back at Isaiah 61. The first thing that Jesus was anointed to do is bring us the Good News of his defeat of sin and its consequences, which is death. Sometimes it is our trials that make us realize we need God. My question for you is simple: "Have you recognized your need for God?"

Have you realized that, like me, you are a sinner—yes a sinner; an imperfect person who misses the mark? Since none of us are perfect that makes every human being a sinner. Sin separates us from God because he is holy and perfect and can't be near sin. But, through the death and resurrection of Jesus Christ, our sins are forgiven and the barrier that separates us from God is removed. We just need to accept his gift of grace. My friends, could it be that God has allowed a test or trial into your life because he wants to begin a personal relationship with you? If you have never opened your heart, or perhaps your mind, to a personal relationship with Jesus, may I ask you, "Why not now?" Just talk to God by repeating this simple prayer:

Lord, I admit that I am not perfect. I make mistakes that I recognize as sin. Thank you so much for Jesus who died on the cross to wipe my mistakes away. I accept your gift of salvation and I invite you to be Lord of my life. I admit that I am powerless in my circumstances. I need your help to make it through difficult times. I'm reaching out for your hand. Thank you for loving me. Help me to live in a way that honors you—even in the tests, trials and tragedies.

In Jesus' Name. Amen

If you just prayed that prayer, welcome to the family! Please tell someone—your leader, a friend, or a pastor—about your decision. They can walk alongside you and support you on your journey of faith.

Assignment Two

The Refining of our Character

It was through hurt and hardship that Ruth's righteous character and faith in God were revealed. The way we walk through the valleys of life will reveal our character strengths and weaknesses. We have learned that *God causes everything to work together for the good of those who love God and are called according to his purpose for them* (Rom. 8:28 NLT). One way good comes out of bad is in our character growth. Remember, life is a university. The time we spend on Earth is only a minute compared with the time we will spend in eternity. We are here to learn to love God, love people, and in the process, become like him. This process of learning and growing will span our lifetime here. The goal is to move from this life to the next mature and complete, lacking nothing (See James 1:4).

God is more interested in your character than he is your comfort. In fact, in Scripture he is referred to as a refiner. Psalm 66:10 says:

10   *For you, O God, tested us; you refined us like silver.* (NIV)

A refiner's job is to purify precious metals by burning out the dross, or impurities. For example, a silversmith will use extreme heat to burn the impurities out of silver. The dross will separate from the silver and then can be drained off. The silversmith knows his work is finished when he can see his reflection in the silver. So it is with us. In God's hand our trials become opportunities to burn away the dross in our character until only his reflection remains.

1.   Read 1 Peter 1:3–7:

> 3   *Let us give thanks to the God and Father of our Lord Jesus Christ! Because of his great mercy he gave us new life by raising Jesus Christ from death. This fills us with a living hope,*
>
> 4   *and so we look forward to possessing the rich blessings that God keeps for his people. He keeps them for you in heaven, where they cannot decay or spoil or fade away.*
>
> 5   *They are for you, who through faith are kept safe by God's power for the salvation which is ready to be revealed at the end of time.*
>
> 6   *Be glad about this, even though it may now be necessary for you to be sad for a while because of the many kinds of trials you suffer.*
>
> 7   *Their purpose is to prove that your faith is genuine. Even gold, which can be destroyed, is tested by fire; and so your faith, which is much more precious than gold, must also be tested, so that it may endure. Then you will receive praise and glory and honor on the Day when Jesus Christ is revealed.* (GNT)

What does our new life in Christ fill us with according to verse 3? Explain in your own words what you think this means.

2.   It has been said that we need hope to cope. How does hope help you in the midst of your trials?

3. What is the purpose of suffering (vs. 7)?

4. In your opinion, what is genuine faith? See Hebrews 11:1 for help.

5. Why do you think is it important to God that our faith endures? See Hebrews 11:6 for help.

> To **endure** means to undergo (as a hardship) especially without giving in: SUFFER.

6. According to 1 Peter 4:12–13, how common are tests, trials and tragedies?

    12   *Beloved, do not be surprised at the fiery ordeal among you, which comes upon you for your testing, as though some strange thing were happening to you;*

    13   *but to the degree that you share the sufferings of Christ, keep on rejoicing, so that also at the revelation of His glory you may rejoice with exultation.*

7. What does the phrase *"that you share the sufferings of Christ"* (1 Peter 4:13) mean to you?

8. According to Romans 5:3–5, what does suffering produce in our lives?

    3   *Not only so, but we also rejoice in our sufferings, because we know that suffering produces perseverance;*

    4   *perseverance, character; and character, hope.*

    5   *And hope does not disappoint us, because God has poured out his love into our hearts by the Holy Spirit, whom he has given us.* (NIV)

    •   How have you seen that are you different as a result of your sufferings?

    •   If you had the power to go back in time and change or erase an experience, but lose the character growth and faith you gained as a result, would you change it? Why or why not?

    > *Blessed is a man who perseveres under trial; for once he has been approved, he will receive the crown of life which the Lord has promised to those who love Him.*
    > James 1:12

Something to Think About:

There is something good that can come from our pain and suffering. Growth, at times, involves pain. While we would never choose the pain for ourselves, God allows it to refine our character. It is in our tests, trials, and even tragedies that we learn we can depend and lean on God. My prayer for you is that, while you do not want to suffer, you understand that God will use the experience to make you more like his son. May you learn to look up to him and not out at your circumstances. Keep your eyes fixed on the author and finisher of your faith. Practice talking to God about what you're going through and trust him to see you through it.

Look up not out!

Assignment Three

Beyond What We See

Isaiah 64:4 says:

> 4   *Since ancient times no one has heard, no ear has perceived, no eye has seen any God besides you, who acts on behalf of those who wait for him.* (NIV)

There is more to our circumstances than we can see. We can only see how the test, trial or tragedy affects us in the here and now. But if we could have a God's-eye view of our experiences, we would see how God works everything for good. Not so sure? Let's take one last look together at Ruth.

1.   Read Ruth 4:17–22:

> 17   *The neighbor women gave him a name, saying, "A son has been born to Naomi!" So they named him Obed. He is the father of Jesse, the father of David.*
>
> 18   *Now these are the generations of Perez: to Perez was born Hezron,*
>
> 19   *and to Hezron was born Ram, and to Ram, Amminadab,*
>
> 20   *and to Amminadab was born Nahshon, and to Nahshon, Salmon,*
>
> 21   *and to Salmon was born Boaz, and to Boaz, Obed,*
>
> 22   *and to Obed was born Jesse, and to Jesse, David.*

• Why do you think the genealogy of Obed was included in Ruth?

• How does this passage demonstrate the victory that can come from trials?

• Who was Obed's grandson (Ruth 4:17)?

2.   Read Matthew 1:1–16:

   1   *The record of the genealogy of Jesus the Messiah, the son of David, the son of Abraham:*

   2   *Abraham was the father of Isaac, Isaac the father of Jacob, and Jacob the father of Judah and his brothers.*

   3   *Judah was the father of Perez and Zerah by Tamar, Perez was the father of Hezron, and Hezron the father of Ram.*

   4   *Ram was the father of Amminadab, Amminadab the father of Nahshon, and Nahshon the father of Salmon.*

   5   *Salmon was the father of Boaz by Rahab, Boaz was the father of Obed by Ruth, and Obed the father of Jesse.*

   6   *Jesse was the father of David the king. David was the father of Solomon by Bathsheba who had been the wife of Uriah.*

   7   *Solomon was the father of Rehoboam, Rehoboam the father of Abijah, and Abijah the father of Asa.*

   8   *Asa was the father of Jehoshaphat, Jehoshaphat the father of Joram, and Joram the father of Uzziah.*

   9   *Uzziah was the father of Jotham, Jotham the father of Ahaz, and Ahaz the father of Hezekiah.*

   10 *Hezekiah was the father of Manasseh, Manasseh the father of Amon, and Amon the father of Josiah.*

   11 *Josiah became the father of Jeconiah and his brothers, at the time of the deportation to Babylon.*

   12 *After the deportation to Babylon: Jeconiah became the father of Shealtiel, and Shealtiel the father of Zerubbabel.*

   13 *Zerubbabel was the father of Abihud, Abihud the father of Eliakim, and Eliakim the father of Azor.*

   14 *Azor was the father of Zadok, Zadok the father of Achim, and Achim the father of Eliud.*

   15 *Eliud was the father of Eleazar, Eleazar the father of Matthan, and Matthan the father of Jacob.*

   16 *Jacob was the father of Joseph the husband of Mary, by whom Jesus was born, who is called the Messiah.*

•   Who was eventually born from Ruth's family line (Matt. 1:16)?

•   What does the family line of Ruth and Boaz teach you about God's greater purpose and plan for your life?

3.   Who are the women listed in the genealogy of Jesus?

What do you know about them? If you can, describe them. If you have an interest in finding more information about them, consider looking them up in a Bible dictionary.

4.   As you think back on your own difficult life experiences, what encouragement do Naomi and Ruth's lives offer you?

Obed, the child of Boaz and Ruth, was an ancestor to Jesus. There was no way the heartbroken Naomi or Ruth could have known that God would use their tragedies for such an amazing purpose. How could they have known that the Messiah would be born into the world through their family line? There was no way for them to know that through the death of their husbands, the loss of their home, and their poverty, God was weaving their pain into his plan to redeem all of mankind. Ruth and Boaz's faithfulness benefited future generations. Understand this all-important point: we may never see the end result of God working all things for our good, but we can trust that he is faithful to his word.

Something to Think About:

Don't you sometimes wish you could have a God's-eye view of your life? I sometimes imagine myself soaring high above the tests, trials, tragedies, and triumphs of life and being able to see the "lay of the land," so to speak. To have a God's-eye perspective is to be able to see how each event lays into the landscape of your life and your future.

I don't know what difficulty or challenge you are facing, but I want you to know that God has a plan for you in it. I can openly say to you that right now in my family we are experiencing a difficult trial. I can't help but wonder why God has allowed it, but none-the-less here it is. I want to say that I'm walking it well, but, honestly, some days I forget to look up to him instead of out at my circumstances. When that happens I feel frustrated, anxious, and even angry. Funny how as a teacher I often teach about what I need most! But I know, that I know, God intends to use this trial for the benefit of my family, not for our harm. Not that the journey won't be difficult, but in the end it will be worth it because my family's faith will grow, my character will mature, and the depth of intimacy in my relationship with God will increase. I also know this process will take time. I refuse to allow bitterness to seep in. Instead, I choose to push in closer to Christ and trust that all my days were ordained for me before one of them came to be.

Wrapping it Up:

Sweet ones, what a journey we have been on together! My prayer for all of you is that you gain a right perspective on your tests, trials and tragedies. I pray that you have learned what it means to walk through each experience with your eyes firmly fixed on God. I pray that, through your trials, your character is shown to be that of a woman of excellence. Most of all, I hope you have learned that you can depend on your kinsman-redeemer—Jesus—to be there for you as you walk through life's ups and downs. I pray that you graduate from UROC at the top of your class.

Now may *The LORD bless you, and keep you; The LORD make His face shine on you, And be gracious to you; The LORD lift up His countenance on you, And give you peace* (Num. 6:24–26).

In the Name of the Father, the Son, and the Holy Spirit. Amen

Study Group Questions

1. What do you think the women of Bethlehem unknowingly hinted would become a blessing to Naomi in future generations? See Ruth 4:16–17 and Matthew 1:1, 5–6a for help.

2. How have we been affected by Boaz's faithfulness to God's instructions for his people? See Ruth 4:14–17 and Matthew 1:1, 5–6a.

3. How can God use our endurance and faith through difficulties to bless future generations?

4. What was the most significant truth you learned in this lesson?

5. What stands out to you as the most significant truth you learned in this study?

NOTES

APPENDIX A:

Observation Sheet

Book of Ruth

Chapter 1

1 Now it came about in the days when the judges governed, that there was a famine in the land. And a certain man of Bethlehem in Judah went to sojourn in the land of Moab with his wife and his two sons.

2 The name of the man was Elimelech, and the name of his wife, Naomi; and the names of his two sons were Mahlon and Chilion, Ephrathites of Bethlehem in Judah. Now they entered the land of Moab and remained there.

3 Then Elimelech, Naomi's husband, died; and she was left with her two sons.

4 They took for themselves Moabite women as wives; the name of the one was Orpah and the name of the other Ruth. And they lived there about ten years.

5 Then both Mahlon and Chilion also died, and the woman was bereft of her two children and her husband.

6 Then she arose with her daughters-in-law that she might return from the land of Moab, for she had heard in the land of Moab that the Lord had visited His people in giving them food.

7   So she departed from the place where she was, and her two daughters-in-law with her; and they went on the way to return to the land of Judah.

8   And Naomi said to her two daughters-in-law, "Go, return each of you to her mother's house. May the Lord deal kindly with you as you have dealt with the dead and with me.

9   "May the Lord grant that you may find rest, each in the house of her husband." Then she kissed them, and they lifted up their voices and wept.

10   And they said to her, "No, but we will surely return with you to your people."

11   But Naomi said, "Return, my daughters. Why should you go with me? Have I yet sons in my womb, that they may be your husbands?

12   "Return, my daughters! Go, for I am too old to have a husband. If I said I have hope, if I should even have a husband tonight and also bear sons,

13   would you therefore wait until they were grown? Would you therefore refrain from marrying? No, my daughters; for it is harder for me than for you, for the hand of the Lord has gone forth against me."

14   And they lifted up their voices and wept again; and Orpah kissed her mother-in-law, but Ruth clung to her.

15   Then she said, "Behold, your sister-in-law has gone back to her people and her gods; return after your sister-in-law."

16   But Ruth said, "Do not urge me to leave you or turn back from following you; for where you go, I will go, and where you lodge, I will lodge. Your people shall be my people, and your God, my God.

17   "Where you die, I will die, and there I will be buried. Thus may the Lord do to me, and worse, if anything but death parts you and me."

18   When she saw that she was determined to go with her, she said no more to her.

19   So they both went until they came to Bethlehem. And when they had come to Bethlehem, all the city was stirred because of them, and the women said, "Is this Naomi?"

20   She said to them, "Do not call me Naomi; call me Mara, for the Almighty has dealt very bitterly with me.

21   "I went out full, but the Lord has brought me back empty. Why do you call me Naomi, since the Lord has witnessed against me and the Almighty has afflicted me?"

22   So Naomi returned, and with her Ruth the Moabitess, her daughter-in-law, who returned from the land of Moab. And they came to Bethlehem at the beginning of barley harvest.

Chapter 2

1   Now Naomi had a kinsman of her husband, a man of great wealth, of the family of Elimelech, whose name was Boaz.

2   And Ruth the Moabitess said to Naomi, "Please let me go to the field and glean among the ears of grain after one in whose sight I may find favor." And she said to her, "Go, my daughter."

3   So she departed and went and gleaned in the field after the reapers; and she happened to come to the portion of the field belonging to Boaz, who was of the family of Elimelech.

4   Now behold, Boaz came from Bethlehem and said to the reapers, "May the Lord be with you." And they said to him, "May the Lord bless you."

5   Then Boaz said to his servant who was in charge of the reapers, "Whose young woman is this?"

6   The servant in charge of the reapers replied, "She is the young Moabite woman who returned with Naomi from the land of Moab.

7   "And she said, 'Please let me glean and gather after the reapers among the sheaves.' Thus she came and has remained from the morning until now; she has been sitting in the house for a little while."

8 Then Boaz said to Ruth, "Listen carefully, my daughter. Do not go to glean in another field; furthermore, do not go on from this one, but stay here with my maids.

9 "Let your eyes be on the field which they reap, and go after them. Indeed, I have commanded the servants not to touch you. When you are thirsty, go to the water jars and drink from what the servants draw."

10 Then she fell on her face, bowing to the ground and said to him, "Why have I found favor in your sight that you should take notice of me, since I am a foreigner?"

11 Boaz replied to her, "All that you have done for your mother-in-law after the death of your husband has been fully reported to me, and how you left your father and your mother and the land of your birth, and came to a people that you did not previously know.

12 "May the Lord reward your work, and your wages be full from the Lord, the God of Israel, under whose wings you have come to seek refuge."

13 Then she said, "I have found favor in your sight, my lord, for you have comforted me and indeed have spoken kindly to your maidservant, though I am not like one of your maidservants."

14 At mealtime Boaz said to her, "Come here, that you may eat of the bread and dip your piece of bread in the vinegar." So she sat beside the reapers; and he served her roasted grain, and she ate and was satisfied and had some left.

15 When she rose to glean, Boaz commanded his servants, saying, "Let her glean even among the sheaves, and do not insult her.

16 "Also you shall purposely pull out for her some grain from the bundles and leave it that she may glean, and do not rebuke her."

17 So she gleaned in the field until evening. Then she beat out what she had gleaned, and it was about an ephah of barley.

18 She took it up and went into the city, and her mother-in-law saw what she had gleaned. She also took it out and gave Naomi what she had left after she was satisfied.

19   *Her mother-in-law then said to her, "Where did you glean today and where did you work? May he who took notice of you be blessed." So she told her mother-in-law with whom she had worked and said, "The name of the man with whom I worked today is Boaz."*

20   *Naomi said to her daughter-in-law, "May he be blessed of the Lord who has not withdrawn his kindness to the living and to the dead." Again Naomi said to her, "The man is our relative, he is one of our closest relatives."*

21   *Then Ruth the Moabitess said, "Furthermore, he said to me, 'You should stay close to my servants until they have finished all my harvest.'"*

22   *Naomi said to Ruth her daughter-in-law, "It is good, my daughter, that you go out with his maids, so that others do not fall upon you in another field."*

23   *So she stayed close by the maids of Boaz in order to glean until the end of the barley harvest and the wheat harvest. And she lived with her mother-in-law.*

Chapter 3

1   *Then Naomi her mother-in-law said to her, "My daughter, shall I not seek security for you, that it may be well with you?*

2   *"Now is not Boaz our kinsman, with whose maids you were? Behold, he winnows barley at the threshing floor tonight.*

3   *"Wash yourself therefore, and anoint yourself and put on your best clothes, and go down to the threshing floor; but do not make yourself known to the man until he has finished eating and drinking.*

4   *"It shall be when he lies down, that you shall notice the place where he lies, and you shall go and uncover his feet and lie down; then he will tell you what you shall do."*

5   *She said to her, "All that you say I will do."*

6   *So she went down to the threshing floor and did according to all that her mother-in-law had commanded her.*

7   When Boaz had eaten and drunk and his heart was merry, he went to lie down at the end of the heap of grain; and she came secretly, and uncovered his feet and lay down.

8   It happened in the middle of the night that the man was startled and bent forward; and behold, a woman was lying at his feet.

9   He said, "Who are you?" And she answered, "I am Ruth your maid. So spread your covering over your maid, for you are a close relative."

10 Then he said, "May you be blessed of the Lord, my daughter. You have shown your last kindness to be better than the first by not going after young men, whether poor or rich.

11 "Now, my daughter, do not fear. I will do for you whatever you ask, for all my people in the city know that you are a woman of excellence.

12 "Now it is true I am a close relative; however, there is a relative closer than I.

13 "Remain this night, and when morning comes, if he will redeem you, good; let him redeem you. But if he does not wish to redeem you, then I will redeem you, as the Lord lives. Lie down until morning."

14 So she lay at his feet until morning and rose before one could recognize another; and he said, "Let it not be known that the woman came to the threshing floor."

15 Again he said, "Give me the cloak that is on you and hold it." So she held it, and he measured six measures of barley and laid it on her. Then she went into the city.

16 When she came to her mother-in-law, she said, "How did it go, my daughter?" And she told her all that the man had done for her.

17 She said, "These six measures of barley he gave to me, for he said, 'Do not go to your mother-in-law empty-handed.' "

18 Then she said, "Wait, my daughter, until you know how the matter turns out; for the man will not rest until he has settled it today."

Chapter 4

1 Now Boaz went up to the gate and sat down there, and behold, the close relative of whom Boaz spoke was passing by, so he said, "Turn aside, friend, sit down here." And he turned aside and sat down.

2 He took ten men of the elders of the city and said, "Sit down here." So they sat down.

3 Then he said to the closest relative, "Naomi, who has come back from the land of Moab, has to sell the piece of land which belonged to our brother Elimelech.

4 "So I thought to inform you, saying, 'Buy it before those who are sitting here, and before the elders of my people. If you will redeem it, redeem it; but if not, tell me that I may know; for there is no one but you to redeem it, and I am after you.' " And he said, "I will redeem it."

5 Then Boaz said, "On the day you buy the field from the hand of Naomi, you must also acquire Ruth the Moabitess, the widow of the deceased, in order to raise up the name of the deceased on his inheritance."

6 The closest relative said, "I cannot redeem it for myself, because I would jeopardize my own inheritance. Redeem it for yourself; you may have my right of redemption, for I cannot redeem it."

7 Now this was the custom in former times in Israel concerning the redemption and the exchange of land to confirm any matter: a man removed his sandal and gave it to another; and this was the manner of attestation in Israel.

8 So the closest relative said to Boaz, "Buy it for yourself." And he removed his sandal.

9 Then Boaz said to the elders and all the people, "You are witnesses today that I have bought from the hand of Naomi all that belonged to Elimelech and all that belonged to Chilion and Mahlon.

10 "Moreover, I have acquired Ruth the Moabitess, the widow of Mahlon, to be my wife in order to raise up the name of the deceased on his inheritance, so that the name of the deceased will not be cut off from his brothers or from the court of his birth place; you are witnesses today."

11   All the people who were in the court, and the elders, said, "We are witnesses. May the Lord make the woman who is coming into your home like Rachel and Leah, both of whom built the house of Israel; and may you achieve wealth in Ephrathah and become famous in Bethlehem.

12   "Moreover, may your house be like the house of Perez whom Tamar bore to Judah, through the offspring which the Lord will give you by this young woman."

13   So Boaz took Ruth, and she became his wife, and he went in to her. And the Lord enabled her to conceive, and she gave birth to a son.

14   Then the women said to Naomi, "Blessed is the Lord who has not left you without a redeemer today, and may his name become famous in Israel.

15   "May he also be to you a restorer of life and a sustainer of your old age; for your daughter-in-law, who loves you and is better to you than seven sons, has given birth to him."

16   Then Naomi took the child and laid him in her lap, and became his nurse.

17   The neighbor women gave him a name, saying, "A son has been born to Naomi!" So they named him Obed. He is the father of Jesse, the father of David.

18   Now these are the generations of Perez: to Perez was born Hezron,

19   and to Hezron was born Ram, and to Ram, Amminadab,

20   and to Amminadab was born Nahshon, and to Nahshon, Salmon,

21   and to Salmon was born Boaz, and to Boaz, Obed,

22   and to Obed was born Jesse, and to Jesse, David.

APPENDIX B:

Be Courageous—Lesson Six

Psalm 27:14

Wait for the Lord; Be strong and let your heart take courage; Yes, wait for the Lord.

Psalm 30:5

For His anger is but for a moment, His favor is for a lifetime;
Weeping may last for the night, But a shout of joy comes in the morning.

Isaiah 43:2

When you pass through the waters, I will be with you; And through the rivers,
they will not overflow you. When you walk through the fire,
you will not be scorched, Nor will the flame burn you.

1 Peter 4:12–13

Beloved, do not be surprised at the fiery ordeal among you, which comes upon you for your testing, as though some strange thing were happening to you; but to the degree that you share the sufferings of Christ, keep on rejoicing, so that also at the revelation of His glory you may rejoice with exultation.

Romans 8:28

And we know that God causes all things to work together for good to those who love God, to those who are called according to His purpose.

Romans 8:37–39

But in all these things we overwhelmingly conquer through Him who loved us. For I am convinced that neither death, nor life, nor angels, nor principalities, nor things present, nor things to come, nor powers, nor height, nor depth, nor any other created thing, will be able to separate us from the love of God, which is in Christ Jesus our Lord.

Isaiah 41:10

"Do not fear, for I am with you; Do not anxiously look about you, for I am your God. I will strengthen you, surely I will help you, Surely I will uphold you with My righteous right hand."

Philippians 4:13

I can do all things through Him who strengthens me.

Psalm 31:24

Be strong and let your heart take courage, All you who hope in the Lord.

Isaiah 40:31

Yet those who wait for the Lord Will gain new strength; They will mount up with wings like eagles, They will run and not get tired, They will walk and not become weary.

Philippians 4:6–8

Be anxious for nothing, but in everything by prayer and supplication with thanksgiving let your requests be made known to God. 7And the peace of God, which surpasses all comprehension, will guard your hearts and your minds in Christ Jesus. 8Finally, brethren, whatever is true, whatever is honorable, whatever is right, whatever is pure, whatever is lovely, whatever is of good repute, if there is any excellence and if anything worthy of praise, dwell on these things.

Hebrews 13:6

...so that we confidently say, "The lord is my helper, I will not be afraid. What will man do to me?"

APPENDIX C:

Overcoming Fear—Lesson Six

Nothing hinders our lives like fear and anxiety. The best antidote for these overwhelming feelings is Scripture. The Bible encourages us to quote the Word as it is our counselor, our shield, and our sword. Whenever you feel a bout of anxiety, fear or doubt coming upon you, repeat and pray these verses for strength and comfort.

Deuteronomy 3:22

Do not fear them, for the Lord your God is the one fighting for you.

Deuteronomy 6:13

You shall fear only the Lord your God; and you shall worship Him and swear by His name.

Joshua 10:8

The Lord said to Joshua, "Do not fear them, for I have given them into your hands; not one of them shall stand before you."

Joshua 10:25 (NIV)

Joshua said to them, "Do not be afraid; do not be discouraged. Be strong and courageous."

Deuteronomy 31:8

The Lord is the one who goes ahead of you; He will be with you. He will not fail you or forsake you. Do not fear or be dismayed.

1 Samuel 12:24

Only fear the Lord and serve Him in truth with all your heart; for consider what great things He has done for you.

2 Chronicles 20:17

"You need not fight in this battle; station yourselves, stand and see the salvation of the Lord on your behalf, O Judah and Jerusalem." Do not fear or be dismayed; tomorrow go out to face them, for the Lord is with you.

Psalm 23:4

Even though I walk through the valley of the shadow of death, I fear no evil,
for You are with me; Your rod and Your staff, they comfort me.

Psalm 27:3

Though a host encamp against me, My heart will not fear;
Though war arise against me, In spite of this I shall be confident.

Psalm 27:1

The Lord is my light and my salvation; Whom shall I fear?
The Lord is the defense of my life; Whom shall I dread?

Psalm 118:6

The Lord is for me; I will not fear;
What can man do to me?

Matthew 10:26

Therefore do not fear them, for there is nothing concealed that will not be revealed,
or hidden that will not be known.

Luke 12:7

Indeed, the very hairs of your head are all numbered.
Do not fear; you are more valuable than many sparrows.

John 14:27

Peace I leave with you; My peace I give to you; not as the world gives do I give to you.
Do not let your heart be troubled, nor let it be fearful.

Mark 5:36b

Do not be afraid any longer, only believe.

Isaiah 35:4

Say to those with anxious heart,
"Take courage, fear not.
Behold, your God will come with vengeance;
The recompense of God will come,
But He will save you."

Isaiah 41:10

Do not fear, for I am with you;
Do not anxiously look about you, for I am your God.
I will strengthen you, surely I will help you,
Surely I will uphold you with My righteous right hand.

Philippians 4:6

Be anxious for nothing, but in everything by prayer and supplication
with thanksgiving let your requests be made known to God.

Psalm 94:19 (NLT)

When doubts filled my mind, your comfort gave me renewed hope and cheer.

APPENDIX D:

Leader Guide

Welcome to the University of Refining Our Character

Tossed, Tumbled and Still Trusting–A Study in the Book of Ruth

We are so pleased that you have agreed to lead a few people through this important study with us. We will give you all the help we can through the print curriculum and this leader guide.

As the leader of your group it is important that you take time to review and become familiar with the *Using Your Study Guide* located at the beginning of your study guide. This will enable you to help your group members understand what will be expected of them each week. Also, reviewing this *Leader Guide* will help prepare you for any possible difficulties during your group discussion time.

In our study *Tossed, Tumbled and Still Trusting*, over the next nine weeks we will look closely at the Book of Ruth to see God at work refining the character of two fascinating people—Naomi and Ruth.

Preparation for Leading Your Group

1. Pray before starting to work on your lesson. Ask God to make the lesson understandable and personal for you. Give him permission to transform you by showing you how he would have you apply his Word as you study.

2. Complete the lesson early enough in the week that you can review the lesson shortly before your group meets.

3.   Study Group Discussion Options:

*   **Preferred Option:** Consider letting the group members choose the questions they want to answer from each assignment. Do this by addressing each assignment by asking, "Which questions in the assignment was the most meaningful to you and why?" Do this for each assignment. You will be pleasantly surprised at how much fun your members will have sharing what they learned and what God showed them. We encourage you to give this a try.

*   Train your members to mark the questions they want to share as they work through the assignments each week. This will enable them to easily find them when the group is sharing.

*   Use the *Study Group Questions* at the end of each lesson.

*   Choose questions from each assignment that seem most significant to you.

*   Consider which verses you want the group to read aloud together before you ask the questions so they have the context of the questions in mind.

*   Write your own questions that better meet the needs of your group.

4.   Take time praying over the suggested *Study Group Discussion Options* so you know which method you will use and you feel prepared.

Leading the Discussion

Here is a suggestion for leading your group each week:

*   Open your group time with prayer.

*   If you have some new ladies joining you, briefly introduce yourselves.

*   If you intend to use a group commitment/agreement be sure to review that at the first meeting. An understanding of expectations ahead of time can prevent disappointment down the road. As new people join the group, give them a copy of the agreement to keep.

*   Begin your group discussion time by using the method you chose from *Preparation for Leading Your Group*.

*   Be sure to save time for prayer requests and praying together after your discussion of the lesson. If time is short, each of you can pray for your own requests. It is okay to keep your eyes open to write down the requests while prayers are prayed.

In order to manage your time in the group, be sure to set a time limit on how long you will discuss each question or assignment so there is time for prayer before your time together ends.

Leader Guide

Lesson One

In *Lesson One* you'll notice we have named *Lesson One, Prerequisite*. Just as many university classes have prerequisite studies before you can take them, *Tossed, Tumbled and Still Trusting* has a prerequisite too. Before we begin to delve into the Book of Ruth, we need to understand what we can about the times in which the book was written. We need to know where the story takes place and what was going on that caused the book to be written.

As you work through the first assignment, you see that Elimelech and Naomi lived in Bethlehem of Judea in tumultuous times not unlike our times today. This story takes place during the *Era of the Judges*. Commentators describe this era as a time of sin and consequences; a time when the Nation of Israel had lost their connection and commitment to God. *"...there was no king in Israel; every man did what was right in his own eyes"* Judges 17:6.

Understanding the times in which Naomi, Ruth, and Boaz lived helps us to see that God was clearly at work in their lives. This fact alone encourages us that God continues to refine and preserve his people today. Understanding this kind of background information helps us make sense of the events that take place in the story.

As the leader, you should help your members understand the importance of doing some background study before starting to read and understand a book of the Bible. Be sure that you have reviewed all the background information made available to you in the lesson.

ASSIGNMENT ONE: The big idea of this assignment is to understand the times in which Naomi and Elimelech lived in Bethlehem of Judea. It would be a good idea to read Judges 2:10-13, 19-22 with the group before they answer any questions related to *Assignment One*.

Question 5: Some people may not be able to relate the time of the Judges with our times today. It is important that you are welcoming of every response. Others may focus on the time of famine. In our economic downturn people are beginning to feel a sense of lack as the economy is slow to rebound. Others may look around and see that our culture as whole seems to consider the things of God to be unimportant, just as in Naomi's day when people had forgotten the past deeds of God and lived to please themselves. Largely they no longer knew God because parents and grandparents failed to pass on the things of God to their children. We see much of the same today. We see the reality of it as standards of morality are much lower than they were even 30 years ago. Some people will see even greater parallels with today. Be quick to affirm each answer.

ASSIGNMENT TWO: In this assignment we ask the students to read the entire Book of Ruth. Encourage your group members to do this. The book should be read all in one sitting, if possible, as you would read a letter from a friend. The point of doing this is to get a feel for the tone or mood of the book. They should see the whole story all at once and identify who the main characters are, what the main events are, and what the order of events is. They should look for where and when the story took place. They may be able to discover if the book itself reveals any of these things or when these things took place.

During your discussion time, consider enlisting someone to begin keeping a list of questions that remain unanswered each week. Together the group can look for the answers to these questions as the weeks unfold.

Question 5: Looking up words in our English dictionary is a very good Bible study habit. Sometimes the definitions don't produce any surprising thoughts that add insight into the verses. But other times there will be shades of meaning that unlock something really meaningful within a passage. If the students don't own an English dictionary, they are easily available online and they are easy to use. We like dictionary.com; it is easy to remember the URL (website address) and it is easy to use once you are on the site.

ASSIGNMENT THREE: In this assignment we ask the students to use the Book of Ruth *Observation Sheet* in the *Appendix*.

This is a study skill exercise that some students will really enjoy. Read the passages with a pen, colored pencils, or highlighter in hand to mark the words they previously looked up in their English dictionary. This practice can be very helpful to learning more about what the Bible says regarding these words. Going back and jotting down what you learn about famine, gleaning, and redeeming as you move from one reference to another can produce a nice list that often leads to great understanding.

Question 2: This is a "what do you think" question. Don't push anyone to answer it. This question is here to get the students thinking about the purpose of this book. It is not likely that inexperienced Bible students will see the light at the end of this tunnel yet. But over the weeks of study, the answer to this question may begin to dawn on them. For those who find the answer to this question for themselves by the end of this study it will be very exciting indeed.

Application for Review—Question 2: If someone has difficulty with **identifying the timeless principles** within the passages, take a few minutes for the group to share their answers to this question. Then go through this exercise together.

The **timeless principles** can be found by re-reading the verses we look at in the lessons. As you reread the passages, pray and ask God to open your understanding of his timeless principles in these verses. We began our Scripture reading in Judges 2:10-13. Let's start with Judges 2:6-13 and walk through it together to see how to do this. We'll use the New Living Translation for this exercise.

The verse that gives us the most intriguing information is verse 10. Let's read it together paying particular attention to what we have underlined for you.

10 After <u>that generation died</u>, <u>another generation</u> grew up who <u>did not acknowledge the LORD or remember the mighty things he had done for Israel</u>. (NLT)

Look at the words that are underlined again. What happened and what was the result? Who was the generation that died? What principle can we glean from this passage?

The passage says, *that generation died.* What generation? To understand what generation we need the context of the passage. Go back and read Judges 2:6-10 looking for the context of the passage we examined in *Assignment One.*

6 After Joshua sent the people away, each of <u>the tribes</u> left to take possession of the land allotted to them.

7 And the Israelites served the LORD throughout the lifetime of Joshua and the leaders who outlived him— <u>those who had seen all the great things the LORD had done for Israel</u>.

8 Joshua son of Nun, the servant of the Lord, died at the age of 110.

9 They buried him in the land he had been allocated, at Timnath-serah in the hill country of Ephraim, north of Mount Gaash.

10 After <u>that generation died</u>, <u>another generation</u> grew up who <u>did not acknowledge the LORD or remember the mighty things he had done for Israel</u>. (NLT)

What do we learn about these two generations? Why didn't the next generation acknowledge the Lord or remember what he had done for Israel? Think about the answers to those questions and you will know the timeless principle.

The principle for us is, if we fail to tell our children about the Lord our God and Jesus Christ, they too, will grow up not knowing God or acknowledging him or knowing what he has done.

Our students can use this method to discern the timeless principles in all the passages we address over the course of this study.

Lesson Two

Welcome back to the *Tossed, Tumbled and Still Trusting Leader Guide.* We pray that your group discussion last week went well and that you are feeling confident as you prepare to lead your group again this week.

As you prepare for leading your group this week, commit your study and preparation time to the Lord in prayer. It will make all the difference in your confidence and the results with your group.

After praying, go back to the leader notes for the last lesson and review all the suggestions we gave you that pertain to your preparation every week. Then come back here to find some specific help for this lesson.

In *Lesson Two* we see the goal and purpose for why this study centers around a university theme. Be sure you are familiar with the concept of likening our journey in Christ to a time of training in a university. UROC is where our character is refined. Our spiritual growth is a process with many learning experiences. Our goal for this study and the UROC series is to attain a transformed life that reflects the character of Christ. As we examine Naomi and Ruth's lives, we see they dealt with hardships with God's help. As with Naomi and Ruth, God is committed to our growth and we can count on him to complete his work of refining our character.

An important aspect of this lesson is the introduction of our declaration: "The goal of UROC is Christ-likeness in all tests, trials, and tragedies. In order to grow and mature in Christ we must learn to overcome the impulses and desires of the flesh." Remind your group that God has a purpose in the midst of difficult times in our lives.

We begin our study time for this lesson by taking a closer look at the characters and events in the Book of Ruth to discover more about them and what happened in their lives. We also get a glimpse into their spiritual journey as well.

ASSIGNMENT ONE: In this assignment we continue to observe what prompted Elimelech to move his family to Moab. Because God is concerned about developing our character, we will begin to look at possible causes for Elimelech's decision.

Question 1: The important clue to the time when this story took place is in Ruth 1:1, *in the days when the judges ruled* (NIV). In *Lesson One* we looked at what the times of the judges were like. We saw the spiritual (Judges 2:10) and moral (Judges 17:6) condition of the people. The generation that entered the Promised Land had all died and failed to teach the next generation about God and all he did for Israel. As a result, the next generation did not know God. The result was that everyone did whatever seemed right in their own eyes. The Israelites no longer trusted God to meet their needs.

Question 7: If questions arise about this question, direct the student's attention back to the meaning of the words, "sojourn" and "remained." The big idea here is that when Elimelech and Naomi left Bethlehem of Judah, their intention was to make a temporary move. However, once in Moab, life was established there for probably 10 years. We can only guess why they remained in Moab. We can speculate that once established there they became comfortable, or making the move back to their homeland was delayed for one reason or another and before they knew it the years went by. Regardless, they continued to live far from God's intended home for them.

ASSIGNMENT TWO: Elimelech and Naomi experienced very difficult times in Bethlehem. They were also living in the times of the Judges when people did what was right in their own eyes and did not know the Lord. Today, we'll examine the reasons for the family's need to leave Bethlehem. Keep in mind the spiritual and moral condition of the people during the time of the Judges as you think through your answers for *Assignment Two*.

Question 2: Your group could have a variety of responses to this question depending on how they relate to it. Many will simply see that the famine (lack of food) caused them to leave. Others may see that their sons were not robust. Elimelech and Naomi may have feared that the boys might not survive a famine. Another possibility is the spiritual condition of the Israelites (Judges 2:10) during the time they lived, may have been a factor. If they were of the generation that did not know of the good things God had done for Israel, they might not have had a strong sense of dependence on God. Also the tendency of everyone doing what was right in their own eyes would strengthen this point of view. If those who knew God and had witnessed all he did for Israel had taught those things through the generations, Elimelech and Naomi may have understood that God would provide and meet their needs. In that case, maybe they would have remained in Bethlehem of Judea trusting God to care for their family.

Question 3: This question has the potential of helping your group members discover a timeless principle that can produce life and death results. If the group fails to see why the Israelites were in the shape they were in spiritually, take them back to your exercise in the leader notes for last week in *Assignment Three*. If you took advantage of that exercise last week your group may be quick to point out what the consequences can be for us today if we fail to tell our children about the Lord. People who don't remember the deeds of the Lord and have never been told about him are not likely to trust him for anything. Today, if someone hasn't been told or seen evidence that God cares for them, they will not be able to embrace him as their savior. It is our responsibility as Christians to make certain our children have heard the truth about God. We are not responsible for the result, only for telling them.

ASSIGNMENT THREE: The goal of UROC is to develop Christ-likeness as a result of growing through our tests, trials and tragedies. In order to grow and mature in Christ we must learn to overcome the impulses and desires of the flesh. In this assignment we see the importance of overcoming when faced with difficulties. The *Word Study* in question 4 can provide understanding about what it means to overcome. This understanding can help us make the connection between overcoming and facing hard times.

Question 1: This question gives you the opportunity to observe what happened in Naomi's life and how her character measured up under fire.

Question 2: Here we take time to evaluate our own experiences and what we are able to learn about ourselves and our character. If your group struggles with these questions you may consider sharing your own thoughts about your life to help them relate. Keep in mind, if your group is not well bonded, this may not be a wise choice for group discussion since it is quite personal. If you do use this question, don't go around the table asking everyone to share. Ask for volunteers; one or two people sharing is sufficient to get the idea of how we can learn and grow through our experiences.

Question 6: A careful reading of Deuteronomy 6:6-12 can help group members understand how they can have consistency as they endeavor to continually remember the Lord. We suggest underlining or making a list of the verbs in the passage. Write out what is said in each instance. They can become clues to successfully overcoming. For example: teach, talk, sit, walk, etc. Each of these verbs gives us a piece of a very good action plan.

Lesson Three

Naomi's life was one with many shattered dreams. In *Lesson Three* we explore the way Naomi responded to the events of her life.

What is in our hearts is revealed by the way we *take,* or respond to our circumstances. It is important to start your study with an attitude of humility and openness before God. Before we begin, pray our theme verse for this lesson.

Search me, O God, and know my heart; test me and know my anxious thoughts. See if there is any offensive way in me, and lead me in the way everlasting. Psalm 139:23-24 (NIV)

ASSIGNMENT ONE: In this lesson we look at what Naomi did well.

Two things Naomi did that are noteworthy:

Question 1: Naomi returned to the land God gave to her people. In Hebrew the word translated "return" is associated with repentance—*the full sense of the word is used to describe a complete change of orientation involving a judgment upon the past and a deliberate redirection for the future.* In light of this information, we believe that Naomi's heart was repentant; she realized that things were not right between her and the Lord. Although she believed that the Lord's hand had gone out against her, she still knew she needed to return to the land of her people, the land God gave to them.

Question 2: Naomi's compassion for her daughters-in-law is evident in Ruth 1:8-9. It is clear from her dialog and prayer that she truly desired for them to be cared for and happily married.

ASSIGNMENT TWO: In *Assignment One* we learned that Naomi did two things well. She returned to the land of her people, Bethlehem of Judah, and she showed compassion for her daughters-in-law, truly desiring the best for them.

In reading through Ruth 1:12-13 we see Naomi's heart as she urged Ruth and Orpah to return to Moab and their families. Here we begin to see characteristics in her heart that needed work.

Question 1: Naomi had clearly <u>lost hope</u>; she lost hope that God would meet Ruth and Orpah's needs in Bethlehem of Judah.

Question 4: In this question, be willing to let the student's voice their thoughts about what Naomi was trusting in (instead of trusting in God to meet their needs). One idea could be that she put her hope in people, but when she realized that people fail, she lost hope. Some may think that because she was not fully convinced that God was working on her behalf she couldn't trust him to meet their needs and therefore she was <u>hopeless</u>, without hope that their needs could be met. Some may think that she didn't put her trust in anything; she panicked and that is why she sent her daughters-in-law back home. Be open to letting people share their thoughts, this is a "What do you *think?*" question.

Question 5: The connection we see between knowing God and having hope is simply that it is very difficult to have hope in the Lord if you don't really know him. It is in knowing God's character, his promises, and his faithfulness that we can grow in our ability to trust him.

Hebrews 12:2 contains a great truth that enables us to gain the hope in God that we so desperately need. *Let us fix our eyes on Jesus, the author and perfecter of our faith....*

ASSIGNMENT THREE: In Ruth 1:19–22, as Naomi arrived in Bethlehem of Judah, she encountered some women who knew her. When the women asked, *"Is this Naomi?"* she replied in verse 21, *"I went out full, but the Lord has brought me back empty."*

Question 1: Naomi means *pleasant*. It seems that was she was so changed by bitterness that she no longer resembled her previously pleasant personality and demeanor. This is a "What do you *think?*" question, so be willing to let the students voice their thoughts. Naomi requested that the women call her Mara, which means *bitter*. We can only guess that Naomi was very aware that she was not the same woman who left there years before.

The Application for Review: The purpose of this sequence of questions is to help us walk through a time of self-examination and personal accountability. Encourage your group to prayerfully work through the exercise, trusting God to help them remember, and be open to letting him heal their hurts and emptiness.

Lesson Four

In *Lesson Three* we saw Naomi without hope, bitter and faithless, returning to Bethlehem of Judah with Ruth. She left Judah full, but returned empty. But God was at work refining Naomi's character; he would not leave her empty. In order to better understand how God would mold Naomi's character, it is helpful to better understand God's character.

ASSIGNMENT ONE: The first aspect of God's character we need to understand, is that God is sovereign; he is in control. A very important lesson for us to learn in this assignment is, *when God allows tests and trials in our lives we must never forget that through it all he is in complete control.* He is in complete control, but don't forget God's actions will never violate his character. From time to time even mature believers struggle with the truth that God is sovereign and good at the same time, but ultimately knowing that both are true gives us the confidence and comfort we need.

Question 1: Give careful attention to the definition of *Sovereign* from a dictionary. Frequently we think we understand what a word means but we aren't very clear about all the implications of the words in the English language. Make a habit of looking up words in a dictionary for greater understanding of Scripture.

Question 3: Some students may struggle with the reality that God can be glorified while evil still exists in our world. Even if you don't struggle with it, as a Christian you are likely to be questioned about this concept from time to time. Some ideas that may arise could be:

You may see that God is glorified when he overcomes evil, based on Ephesians 1:14. The most important example in Scripture of God overcoming evil is seen when Jesus went to the cross to die and pay the price for our sins. Ultimately, Jesus overcame evil at the cross; sin no longer has the power of death. That means if we believe and accept his sacrifice on our behalf, Jesus' death restores our relationship with God and our sins are no longer held against us—our sins and mistakes are forgiven, and we are made right with God.

Although God has not removed evil from our world altogether, Jesus' death did conquer it. We don't see it in our daily experience, but the fact remains that it is true. As you consider this question, you may see that God does have a plan to deal with evil in the end, based on Proverbs 16:4. This verse also implies that God has a purpose in everything. You may find Romans 8:28 helpful: *And we know that God causes everything to work together for the good of those who love God and are called according to his purpose for them.* (We will spend more time with this verse in *Assignment Three.*) When the tough things in life turn out for good, God is glorified.

Also in John 16:33, we have assurance that Jesus has overcome the world. God gave us the Scriptures to help us understand everything we need to know. When Jesus said, *"I have overcome the world"* he means he overcame evil too. Make no mistake, when Jesus overcame the world, God was glorified. When one person accepts God's plan through Jesus Christ, God is glorified.

Question 6, Second Bullet: Consider Job 2:9-10, *"...Shall we indeed accept good from God and not accept adversity?" In all this Job did not sin with his lips.* Why? Job knew God. He trusted him. The fact that Job did not curse God showed his total love and trust in God.

ASSIGNMENT TWO: The most important thing we need to keep in mind as we move into this assignment is that God isn't the author of evil. If that were so, God would not be holy. But God *is* holy and sin is present by God's consent, he did not create it. We have the choice or option to sin but it is not of God's choosing that we do sin. The gift of our free will allows us to make choices that can produce evil just as our free will can make choices that produce good. In this assignment we look at God's goodness as seen through his actions toward us; we use Psalm 103:1–18 as our text.

Question 1: As you begin this assignment we ask you to circle every reference, either stated or implied, to God's goodness in this passage. This practice of circling or underlining different aspects of verses helps us to more carefully observe what the passage says. After circling all you see, it is quite revealing to go back and make a list of all the things the passage says about God's goodness. Sometimes these truths about God can be eye-opening. If you have difficulty identifying the good things, watch for the verbs—the action words—in the passage.

Question 1, Second Bullet: In order to come up with your own ideas to help you intentionally praise God daily, consider things like:

1. Take a minute or two at the end of the day to record things you are grateful for, then give God thanks and glory (recognition) for what he did for you.

2. Call, text, e-mail, or tell someone in person something God did for you that day.

3. Make a point of praying at the end of the day with your children and help them recall the good things God did over the course of the day.

Question 4: Keep in mind that some of us have good relationships with our fathers and others don't; this can influence the way we feel about God as a father. Seeing God as the perfect loving father who is always good and has our best interests foremost in his mind, can offer us a healthy perspective of the character of God. We can trust him to always work toward what is ultimately best for us even if we can't see it at the moment.

Question 5: The fill-ins are "punish us" and "harshly."

ASSIGNMENT THREE: Naomi didn't understand why she suffered all the things she did. But she did know she needed to return to the land of God's people. In spite of her despair Naomi did the right thing, she *returned* and God met her right where she was in the midst of her bitterness. There she saw God's goodness working out his purpose for her life—his good purpose for her life.

In this assignment we highlight Naomi and Job's experiences and response to God in the midst of their disasters, pain and suffering. Then we move to Romans and James for more insight concerning where God is when bad things happen.

Question 1: A review of *Assignment One* will refresh your memory about what we learned about Job. If you want more information about Job's story, here is a brief synopsis:

After the tragedy of losing his children and his livelihood, Job faced debilitating illness. Three well-meaning friends came to counsel him. But they were unable to console him because they had no understanding of what was behind Job's suffering. After his friends had their say, Job answered them (Job 26–31). He steadfastly defended his integrity and devotion to God even though he could not explain why he had suffered so much. After Job spoke, a young man rebuked Job's friends for failing to help him understand why he suffered. He offered encouragement to Job reminding him that we don't always know why God allows hardship, but we must trust him (Job 32–37). God answered Job by questioning him instead of offering a defense (Job 38–41). Job responded to God with humility (Job 42:1–6). Finally we see the end of the story; God's goodness and Job's restoration (Job 42:7–17).

Don't spend much time researching Job, unless you have a burning desire to do so. The point of including Job's story is to emphasize his response and the outcome to his troubles and contrast them with Naomi's response and outcome to her troubles. Ultimately we are able to see God's goodness in both situations. Note that this is a "What do you *think*" question?

Question 4: Look at James 1:2–4 below.

2   *Dear brothers and sisters, when troubles come your way, consider it an opportunity for great joy.*

3   *For you know that when your faith is tested, your endurance has a chance to grow.*

4   *So let it grow, for when your endurance is fully developed, you will be perfect and complete, needing nothing.* James 1:2–4 (NLT)

Some people have a really hard time understanding that God's testing is a good thing. The key to understanding this truth is in grasping the truth that God is in control, he is good, he loves you with an everlasting love that will never fail, and he is with you at all times. God is always concerned about our character, desiring the best for each of us. He does not allow difficulties as some sick potentate deriving pleasure from watching us suffer; his pleasure comes from seeing us grow and fulfill his good and perfect purpose for our lives.

Lesson Five

In *Lesson Four* we compared Naomi and Job's circumstances, their response to those circumstances, and their ultimate outcomes. We spent time understanding how the sovereignty of God never contradicts his character. We used Psalm 103:1–18 as our text to appreciate the goodness of God. We also looked at how God is always with us working to grow godly character in us and bring about his good purposes in our lives.

In this lesson we look at the way Ruth responded to the challenges and circumstances of her life. We look closely at three of the six character traits of a consistent over-comer seen in Ruth as she walked through her circumstances.

ASSIGNMENT ONE: The mark of a woman of excellence is seen in the midst of life's challenges; she does not give in to her feelings, she rises above them. This is a result of her faith and faithfulness to God.

You will notice in our text for this assignment, Ruth 1:15-18, we have placed the Strong's Exhaustive Concordance numbers in super-script behind a few words. Below the passage you will find a *Word Studies* box with the Hebrew words defined and identified with the Strong's numbering system. These references are a peek into a process for looking up biblical words used in our English translations of the Bible. Word studies add greater understanding of the intended meaning of the original passages of Scripture.

ASSIGNMENT TWO: In *Assignment One*, we saw Ruth demonstrate the character quality of *faithfulness*. In this assignment we see Ruth affirm her commitment to Naomi using Covenant language which suggested that her *loyalty* to Naomi was until death separated them. Ruth did not make an idle promise to Naomi, she was well aware of the commitment she was making to her.

Question 2: Because Ruth was a Moabite, she wouldn't have been acquainted with the God of Israel. She would not have reliable knowledge of what God had done for them. Our view is that Ruth learned about the God of Israel and what he did for Israel from Naomi. If that is the case, Naomi might not have reflected the mentality of many in Israel during the time of the Judges. In *Lesson One* we learned that the generation who knew God and saw what he had done for Israel died. *After that whole generation had been gathered to their fathers, another generation grew up, who knew neither the LORD nor what he had done for Israel* (Judges 2:10 NIV) and, in Judges 17:6 we read, *In those days there was no king in Israel; every man did what was right in his own eyes.* It appears that Naomi may have introduced Ruth to the God of Israel.

ASSIGNMENT THREE: In our last assignment we saw Ruth's loyalty to Naomi clearly demonstrated through her commitment to remain with Naomi until death separated them. In this assignment we see Ruth's *determination* to begin a new life with Naomi in the land of her people and with her God.

Ruth's determination to care for Naomi's needs and that of four friends who lowered a paralytic through a roof so he could be healed are examples we look at in this assignment. Each was determined to accomplish a task that brought about life-changing results. In Ruth's case, her commitment to overcome her tragic circumstances changed the course of both her life and Naomi's life. The determination of the four friends of the paralytic not only brought about the opportunity for the man to be healed, but all present at the time glorified God (Mark 2:1-12).

Practical Exercise: The *Practical Exercise* is designed to help you put what you learn through your study of Scripture into practice daily. An intellectual understanding of Scripture is not enough; it must change our lives if we are to see character growth that God desires from our time in his Word.

Take time to work through the *Practical Exercise* and be prepared to share your progress with your group at the next meeting.

Lesson Six

In *Lesson Five* we looked at Ruth as a woman of excellence. We saw that a woman of excellence possesses six traits that contributed to her being a consistent over-comer. We took a close look at the first three character traits as demonstrated in Ruth's life: *faithfulness, loyalty,* and *determination.* In *Lesson Six, A Woman of Excellence–Part Two,* we examine the last three character traits of a consistent over-comer: *courage, humility,* and *obedience.*

ASSIGNMENT ONE: When Ruth's husband died, her life took an unexpected turn toward hardship. But when Naomi decided to move back to Bethlehem of Judah there would be many obstacles to overcome. In this assignment we look at Ruth's *courage* to face the unknown ahead and how she courageously embraced a new life with an uncertain future.

For background and greater understanding of what Ruth might have to face when she went to Bethlehem with Naomi, we want to keep in mind the setting and history between Moab and Israel. Not all commentators agree, but for several reasons we believe that Ruth and Naomi lived early in the time of the Judges.

- When Moses sent the spies into Jericho in the Promised Land, Rahab lived there. She and her family were spared and allowed to remain there because of her kindness to the spies. So the men said to her, *"Our life for yours if you do not tell this business of ours; and it shall come about when the LORD gives us the land that we will deal kindly and faithfully with you"* (Josh. 2:14). *However, Rahab the harlot and her father's household and all she had, Joshua spared; and she has lived in the midst of Israel to this day, for she hid the messengers whom Joshua sent to spy out Jericho* (Josh. 6:25).

- Rahab was the mother of Boaz (Matt. 1:5). He most likely knew of Joshua from his mother's stories and may have even known Joshua. The era of the Judges began after Joshua died (Judg. 1:1). Regardless of whether Boaz knew Joshua, there likely wasn't more than a generation between Joshua and the time when Naomi lived in Bethlehem of Judah.

- In his words to Ruth at the threshing floor, Boaz implied that he considered himself to be much older than Ruth. *Then he said, May you be blessed of the LORD, my daughter. You have shown your last kindness to be better than the first by not going after young men, whether poor or rich* (Ruth 3:10).

For these reasons we are confident that the Book of Ruth was set in the early days of the Judges. The Book of Judges records each judge and their conquests in chronological order. Othniel, was Israel's first judge and he ruled for 40 years. Ehud was Israel's second judge. We believe it is safe to assume that Joshua had not been dead for so many years that Boaz could not have been alive during at least part of Joshua's life.

In Judges 3:28 we see Ehud preparing Israel to strike down the Moabites. *He said to them, "Pursue them, for the LORD has given your enemies the Moabites into your hands." So they went down after him...* (Judges 3:28). From these things we conclude that during the time that Naomi was in Moab, the people there were aware of the strife that had existed between Moab and Israel. Even if they were living without war at the time, there were clearly times that Moab was the enemy of Israel and it appears they were never right with the God of Israel as a nation. Ruth was very likely aware of Moab's tumultuous history with Israel, which could have made her decision to live with Naomi in Bethlehem filled with uncertainty.

Question 3: From Ruth 2:2 it appears that Ruth may have been concerned that she wouldn't be allowed to glean in some fields; it is possible that being a Moabite she might not have been welcomed. It would take courage to start out on her own in a foreign land without Naomi at her side.

Question 4: Ruth 2:9 gives insight to possible risks for Ruth's safety. Some ideas might be: Boaz commanded his servants not to touch her; that might indicate that she could be vulnerable to physical harm at the hands of undisciplined men. Work in the fields was hard physical work. Boaz also showed concern for her need to stay hydrated, indicating that she might be overcome from heat or sun exposure.

Question 5: Ruth's biggest obstacle was having no husband. Being a Moabite didn't lend well to finding a suitable husband in Bethlehem. Ruth also needed to care for Naomi and providing for their needs was a primary concern. Courage was required to overcome these obstacles.

ASSIGNMENT TWO: In this assignment we will look at how Ruth showed herself to *be humble*. True humility comes from understanding who God is and who he created us to be. Humble people don't need to downplay or elevate themselves. They are content with the way God created them and experience joy in living out his purposes for their life.

Question 1: Ruth recognized her position within her new culture in Bethlehem; she was a foreigner, a woman, and a poor widow. It is very likely she would not view herself as Boaz's equal. It is reasonable to think that Boaz's words overwhelmed her with awe and gratitude. In her humility she did what she could to bow before him as low as she possibly could, to show her respect and gratitude toward him. Ruth's action also showed a humble, submissive heart and respect for him.

Question 4: Ruth ministered to Naomi and showed compassion for her. She looked out for her interests and provided for her. Ruth had a servant's heart toward Naomi. She met her physical needs such as food, filling up Naomi's physical emptiness. She filled her with good news and awakened hope in Naomi's heart and mind (Ruth 2:17–18).

ASSIGNMENT THREE: Naomi gave Ruth instructions about what she should do; she was quickly *obedient*. Ruth was not only obedient to Naomi's request, but later she was obedient to Boaz as well.

Question 5: Some synonyms for *excellence* are *distinction, perfection, greatness, goodness,* and *quality.* Think about how these words might best describe the way people in Bethlehem may have viewed Ruth.

Practical Exercise: This exercise is designed to offer practical ways we can move past being slaves to our feelings. Instead, we can learn to make choices based on our faith and what we know to be true about God. By responding to our faith, we can make choices that are healthy and lead to life. Encourage your group to complete this exercise.

Question 3: In Hebrews 11:6 we read that God *...rewards those who earnestly seek him* (NIV). It might be helpful to spend some time thinking about what it really means to *earnestly seek* God.

Lesson Seven

In *Lesson Six* we looked at the last three character traits Ruth demonstrated as a consistent overcomer: courage, humility and obedience. In *Lesson Seven*, we begin to look at Boaz and the character of the kinsman-redeemer. Here, we begin to see the character qualities Boaz demonstrated and how Naomi's life began to change as a result of Boaz's role as the protector and provider.

Be sure that your group members have read the introductory information we provided at the beginning of this lesson. It offers some background for understanding the role of the kinsman-redeemer. For more information and background study, consider looking up "kinsman" and "kinsman-redeemer" in a Bible dictionary.

ASSIGNMENT ONE: In this assignment we see *Boaz the protector*. When Ruth told Naomi where she gleaned and whose field it was, Naomi's surprised response leads us to believe that it was God who led Ruth to Boaz's fields.

Question 2: The fill-ins are as follows:

- Boaz provided <u>PHYSICAL</u> protection for young Ruth commanding that the servant not lay a hand on her.
- In verse 15 Boaz provided protection from <u>VERBAL</u> insults.

Question 4: God is willing and able to protect us, but he also requires obedience. Our failure to obey God doesn't override the natural consequences of our disobedience. The results of obedience frequently protect us from harm.

ASSIGNMENT TWO: Here we look at *Boaz the provider*. Naomi and Ruth were poor because they were both widows and without husbands or sons to provide for their needs. As Boaz moved into the role of provider things begin to look better for them.

Important Reminder: Keep in mind that our study of God's Word must be more than intellectual knowledge and understanding. We must allow it to transform our lives. As you study, continually ask God how he desires for you to apply what you are learning; then take time to listen for his direction. We won't hear God if we don't quiet ourselves and listen. Two good questions to ask ourselves as we work through each assignment are: "What is God asking me to do?" and "What am I going to do about it?"

Question 1: Here we asked you to list the physical needs that Boaz provided for Naomi and Ruth. The students may see different things so be open to their thoughts. Some things that may be seen include: water to keep Ruth from being thirsty, food, encouragement to eat until she was satisfied, emotional protection by insisting that his servants not insult or rebuke her, and Boaz instructed the servants to purposely pull out for Ruth some grain for her to gather so she'd have plenty of good grain to take home to Naomi. There may be other things, so be open to a variety of answers.

Questions 3–5: These questions are designed to help students think about how God is at work providing for us on a daily basis, not only when we have a crisis.

ASSIGNMENT THREE: In this assignment we see how Boaz's protection and provision broke down the walls of bitterness that surrounded Naomi—and both she and Ruth found comfort.

Question 2: In Ruth 2:11, Boaz clearly understood that Ruth began doing what she could for Naomi after her own husband died. Although we do not know for certain, it is possible that Ruth did not have much time to grieve the loss of her husband if she took on the role of caregiver for Naomi soon after her husband passed away.

Lesson Eight

Lesson Seven was: *Boaz the Kinsman-redeemer–Part One.* We looked at Boaz the protector and provider. We also began to see Naomi and Ruth begin to hope in a different future as a result of Boaz's care for them. In *Lesson Eight* we will continue to look at the role Boaz played in their lives as he demonstrated himself as their kinsman-redeemer, a promise keeper, and restorer.

ASSIGNMENT ONE: In this assignment we see Boaz take on the role of the kinsman-redeemer on behalf of Ruth and Naomi.

Question 1: When Ruth said to Boaz, *"I am Ruth your maid. So spread your covering over your maid, for you are a close relative"* she was asking him to be her kinsman-redeemer—to take on the responsibility of making her his wife on behalf of her deceased husband. She asked him to redeem what was lost to her, and in turn lost to Naomi—their place in the family, and heirs for their deceased husbands. This also would assure them of the financial support they lacked.

Question 2: In Ezekiel 16:8 we see God promising Israel, or Solomon promising his lover, full commitment to enter into a covenant relationship with them. This was understood to be commitment that was binding unto death. This involved the most obligatory kind of agreement between parties.

Question 5: It seems that Boaz was humbled and honored that Ruth would choose him—a much older man—to take on this very important role on her behalf. His response to her made it clear that he had the utmost respect for her.

ASSIGNMENT TWO: Here we see *Boaz the Promise Keeper*.

Question 2: The land was passed as an inheritance through the generations, Elimelech's name would be lost if the land was not redeemed. If Ruth could secure a kinsman-redeemer for the land, it was expected that he would also marry her (the widow) and provide an heir for Ruth's husband (the deceased, Mahlon). The redemption of the land not only provided an inheritance for the heir, it also provided security for Ruth and Naomi.

Question 3: When a man died and left no male heir, the land could be sold to a kinsman-redeemer. If this didn't happen, the land went to the priest as the representative of Jehovah.

ASSIGNMENT THREE: In this assignment we see *Boaz the Restorer*.

Question 1: The women considered Ruth and Boaz's child to be Naomi's grandchild; verse 17 states this clearly.

Question 2: See *Naomi's Transformation* on page 113 for help.

Question 3: This question may be difficult for those with little Bible background knowledge. If this is the case for some, encourage them to work on question 4 first and then see if any thoughts come to mind.

Question 4: Depending on your group members' familiarity with the New Testament, you may have answers that include Christ's provision of forgiveness and redemption. Some may see more; i.e. he provides us with an inheritance, an eternal homeland in heaven, hope for our future, gives us reason to rejoice, fills us with joy, he is our kinsman-redeemer. Don't discourage additional thoughts. See *Wrapping it Up* for ideas.

Lesson Nine

In *Lesson Eight* we looked at the roles Boaz played in Naomi and Ruth's lives as he demonstrated himself as their kinsman-redeemer, a promise keeper and restorer. In this lesson we explore how the Lord will use our tests, trials and tragedies to refine our character as he fills us with more of himself.

ASSIGNMENT ONE: While we may never know why God has allowed us to go through difficult and painful times, we can be certain that his will is always for our good and not our harm.

Question 1, First Bullet: Depending on the translations used, the answers your group shares may include: the Lord's promises to those who mourn are: comfort, captives released, prisoners freed, crown of beauty for ashes, a joyous blessing, praise instead of despair, and their righteousness will be like great oaks planted for God's glory. The group may enjoy discussing what these things might look like in our everyday circumstances.

Question 1, Fourth Bullet: Experiences to which we give God all the credit for getting us through them or for a good outcome bring glory to God.

Question 2, Second Bullet: Our troubles are an opportunity to respond well. They can build righteous character if we learn to respond in godly ways. At first we may not think our troubles can produce anything good, but by trusting God to work through our circumstances and in our hearts, he will bring about good results and he will be glorified.

Question 2, Third Bullet: *Things unseen.* This refers to things eternal in the spiritual realm; things concerning our true home in the presence of God—heaven and spiritual blessings not earthly blessings.

Question 3: We can live through difficult times with our thoughts and perspective on eternity, not focusing on this temporary life here on Earth.

Question 5: In our humanity we have no righteousness of our own. As we grow and mature spiritually our tests, trials, and tragedies reveal whether or not we are rooted and established in the Lord. When we are seen to be righteous, it is God's righteousness that is seen through us and God gets the glory.

ASSIGNMENT TWO: It was through hurt and hardship that Ruth's righteous character and faith in God were revealed. The way we walk through the valleys of life will reveal our character strengths and weaknesses.

Question 2: Hope gives us perspective and motivates us to persevere through difficulties. Hope is the confidence that God is accomplishing his purposes for us in the midst of our trials.

Question 3: According to 1 Peter 1:7, the purpose of suffering is to prove that your faith is genuine so it may endure and you can receive praise, glory, and honor when Jesus is revealed.

Question 4: According to Hebrews 11:1, *genuine Faith is the confidence that what we hope for will actually happen; it gives us assurance about things we cannot see* (NLT).

Question 5: It is important to God that our faith endures because *...without faith it is impossible to please God, because anyone who comes to him must believe that he exists and that he rewards those who earnestly seek him* (Heb. 11:6 NIV).

Question 7: The suffering referred to in 1 Peter 4:13 is often thought of as persecution of believers in Christ. For additional New Testament verses that speak of suffering with Christ see Romans 8:17; 2 Corinthians 1:5-7; Philippians 3:10; and Acts 16:22-25.

Question 8: The Spirit of God uses suffering to produce god-like character in us. This work is not dependent on our determination and performance; it is God's work in us. The character God develops in us is usually more obvious to others than it is to us.

ASSIGNMENT THREE: We can only see how a test, trial or tragedy affects us in the here and now. But if we could have a God's-eye view of our experiences we would see how God works everything for good.

Question 1, First Bullet: If you don't know why Obed's genealogy was included in the Book of Ruth, hang in there—we will look at this together!

Question 1, Second Bullet: After her sons died, Naomi had no hope of having children or grandchildren. The birth of Obed through Ruth overcame that obstacle and provided for her needs, desires, and future.

Question 2, First Bullet: Jesus was eventually born from Ruth's family line (see Matt. 1:16).

APPENDIX E:

Meet the Authors

Passionate. Transparent. Approachable. Anointed. That's what people say about Bible teacher, speaker, life coach, and author CJ Rapp. She connects with her audiences. It's a heart thing.

Armed with a mission to move women from pain to purpose and purpose to passion, CJ has established Unfading Beauty Ministries, Inc., Infusion Publishing and is co-founder of Trash the Lies women's conferences. She has boldly stepped up to take on the issues women face, tenderly sharing God's truth from his love letter, the Bible. Her passion for God's Word is matched by her desire to see lives transformed by its truth—to know who we are in his sight and how he wants us to live in this mixed up world.

Once a young woman suffering from low self-esteem and the consequences of poor choices, CJ has experienced first-hand God's power to change lives. Gradually, gently, God has transformed her heart, thinking, attitude, and actions. In time, her low self-esteem was exchanged for a rock solid identity in Christ. Encouraged by her husband, John, and sons, Dillon and Austin, she answered God's call and began ministering to women.

God is now using CJ's past experiences to connect her heart with the hearts of women across the nation.

Today, CJ understands the power that words, lies and cultural messages have on a woman's sense of worth. She knows the power of poor past choices to keep a woman from believing God will use her. She comprehends a woman's need for significance in a world that marginalizes her contributions to society. She is tireless in her quest to encourage women to live the abundant, Spirit-filled life.

In addition to speaking to women at conventions, conferences, retreats, and special events across the country, CJ teaches a Bible study class at her home church in Lake Forest, CA.

Her message: "The answers to life's greatest challenges lie in a relationship with God and a love for his Word."

Her commitment: "Helping women see themselves as the beloved, beautiful women they are in God's eyes."

And you will know the truth, and the truth will set you free. John 8:32 (NLT)

Pam's past life experiences give her perspective, insight, and the compassion that enable her to help women as they walk through difficult, unexpected, and trying times of life. Pam understands the disappointments of betrayal, personal failures, divorce and broken families. Her experiences from childhood, teen years, marriage and parenting, personal failures, divorce and remarriage, blended family, and the roles of being a grandparent have given her a platform for speaking into the lives of women in many life stages.

Currently Pam is Project Manager at Infusion Publishing, a ministry of Unfading Beauty Ministries, Inc., a non-profit 501(c)(3). Apart from her work at Infusion Publishing and Unfading Beauty Ministries, Pam's recent ministry includes group leader coaching in a centralized women's Bible study at her home church, Saddleback Church, in Lake Forest, California. Her passion is to help others learn how to study the Bible and discover the transforming power of God's Word.

As an active Bible study curriculum developer for the past 17 years, Pam brings a wealth of experience to draw from. She actively participated with Brett Eastman in the development of Saddleback Church's earliest small group studies. Her efforts included serving on the writing teams for major Saddleback Church campaigns including the world-renowned *40 Days of Purpose*. While serving on staff at the church as Associate Producer, she was involved with the development and production of the *Saddleback Bible Study Series*, small group video-guided print curriculums.

Pam also worked for Lifetogether as a curriculum developer and writer. During her tenure at Lifetogether, Pam assisted with the development and writing of print curriculum for Focus on the Family, Zondervan, Baker Publishing, and Tyndale House. Her Bible curriculum work at Saddleback Church and LifeTogether touched the lives of thousands of individuals and small groups, both nationally and internationally.